The Artemesia Book

The Artemesia Book
POEMS SELECTED AND NEW

Colleen Thibaudeau

Brick Books

CANADIAN CATALOGUING IN PUBLICATION DATA

Thibaudeau, Colleen, 1925-
　The artemesia book

Poems.
ISBN 0-919626-49-1

I. Title.

PS8539.H53A78 1991　　C811'.54　　C91-093751-6
PR9199.3.T452A78 1991

Copyright © Colleen Thibaudeau, 1991
Second printing, October 1997

Some of these poems have appeared in *Air 3*, *Air 14.15.16*, *Alphabet*, *An Anthology of London, Ontario Poets*, *Applegarth's Folly*, *Brick*, *The Canadian Forum*, *Canadian Poems 1850-1952*, *Canadian Poetry*, *Connexions*, *Contemporary Verse*, *The Fiddlehead*, *Forty Women Poets of Canada*, *Made in Canada*, *Northern Review*, *Other Voices*, *Poetry (Chicago)*, *The Tamarack Review*, *The Combined Blewointment Open Picture Book nd th News*, *Twentieth Century Poetry*, and *The Wind Has Wings*.

We acknowledge the support of the Canada Council for the Arts for our publishing programme. The support of the Ontario Arts Council is also gratefully acknowledged.

With thanks to Stan Dragland, John Donlan, and Sue Schenk.

Printed on Zephyr Antique Laid, sewn into signatures and bound by The Porcupine's Quill, Inc., Erin, Ontario.

Brick Books
431 Boler Road, Box 20081
London, Ontario, N6K 4G6

Contents

Sea Gone Girl

Poem as Potato 11
Held Back But Not Exactly Tension What 12
Fishes out of Water 13
By You It's Four O'clock Yesterday 14
Amethysts 15
The Children and the Storm 16
Butterfly Window 19
Throwing a Cigarette into Water 20
A Poem for my Professor 21
It Is a Rainy Day in March 23
Sea Gone Girl 24
The Bellringer 25

My Granddaughters Are Combing Out Their Long Hair

Poem (I do not want only) 29
The Obvious Skies 30
White Bracelets 31
An Afternoon's Teasing … 32
She Wore a Look of Looking 33
The Green Family 34
The Strawberry Bed: a Paradox 36
Blue and Yellow Boy 38
Walk 5 39
So André Gide Was Dead 40
Idea for an Elegy: Finished Up for the Brinks 41
Aristide Bruant au Honey Dew 42
Getting the High Bush Cranberries 43
My Granddaughters Are Combing Out Their Long Hair 45
Lullaby of the Child for the Mother 46
Sunday Morning 47
'It Is As If They Were Never There' 48
Protectiveness 49
I Have Confused the Feeling 52
Neruda Walks In 53

The Brown Family 54
Walk 4 56
King's Park, Manitoba 57
As If In Code ... 62
In Leningrad ... 63
A Shame 64
Song: Six Makes the Set 66
The Rose Family 67
Little Pasternak Poem Promised to Mrs. Neville 68
February 20th 69
This Iron 70
Poem (A feeling of nightfall having been alone all day) 71
Big Trees 72
Spring Poem 73
I had the window open 74
Walk 3 75
Notes on a Day 76
Poem (There's a waterfall in Iceland) 77
The Barbara Suite 78
Aroha's Fossil 79
This Elastic Moment 80

Ten Letters 81

The Martha Landscapes

The Glass Cupboard 97
Last Night I Dreamed 98
My Grandmother's Sugar Shell, Ontario Baroque 99
Malcolm Working 100
A Page of Rage 101
The Blue of the Swimming Pool 102
*Little Anne Running, Big Anne Shopping & Another Anne's
    Mysterious Visiting Birds* 103
Lost Everything, Almost Everything 104
About Noon 106
The Tin Shop 108

A Tree for St. T 110
Inwhich I Realize I Meant To Clean Up My Brother's House
   As A Nice Surprise For When He Came Back
     From His Camp And That I Have Left It A Bit Late 111
The Dieppe Gardens Poems 112
Sociable People Wondering What I Do 113
The Tomato Pickers Observed 115
Beatie's Palaces 116
St. Thomas: the Great Heat Wave of '36 118
Inwhich I Become Confused, the End of the World Being Imminent 120
Parody 1: Margaret Atwood, 'Presolstice' 121
Parody 2: Raymond Souster, 'The Worm' 122
Parody 3: W.W.E. Ross, 'There's a Fire in the Forest' 123
Parody 4: Al Purdy, 'The Rattlesnake' 124
Parody 5: Phyllis Gotlieb, 'Ordinary Moving' 125
from the planned woodlot to the freedom of Mrs. Field 126
The Martha Landscapes 130

The Artemesia Book

Name Dropping As Skipping Stones 137
Listening in Together 138
Childlight Town 139
Inwhich I Put On My Mother's Old Thé Dansant Dress 141
Lines Not For Mona 142
Photo 143
Watermelon Summer 144
Miniatures 145
Inwhich I Meet the Strawberry Shaman
   And The Japonica Bushelful Bountiful Lady 148
Inwhich Tim, Bill And I Discuss The Governor's Road 149
from Throgmoggle and Engestchin: A relationship 151
Throgmoggle and Engestchin & the Bird People 153
Throgmoggle and Engestchin, Having Read the Reviews 154
Throgmoggle and Engestchin Experience An Upsetting Border Crossing 155
Wild Turkeys 157
Fanning Mill into Shredder 158

Race Track Kids 159
The Cooper 160
The Belfast Policeman 161
One-eyed Pierre 162
This Dragon Year Will Eat You Up For Sure 163
What Happened to the N.Y. Sunday Times 164
Running Down to Barachois 165
Looking at The Artemesia Book 168

Notes 171

Biographical Note 172

Sea Gone Girl

Poem as Potato

Deepdown cellar one of
the poems is beginning to sprout!
an *Eye*
an oyster-trim Telecommunication
a filament of Identity-making
Oracular!

Not likely;
Just poor Blind Spot,
Companion to Peg Leg
Of the Order of Heart Felt.
A whole Bagful.

Held Back But Not Exactly Tension What

Held back but not exactly tension what
stirring takes this moment back
to ringleted willows and to simpering pools,
suspends suddenly

whole livingrooms of lifely conversation,
husbands and wives, calm and conjugal,
together-weathering as homesteads
right with fence and crib and stack?

Your soft deciduous old woodsy verve,
o dear priapus unaware,
along with nymph, gay garland, coronal
conjures up images of leaves, of drapery disturbed,

of sudden fear and flight
into the trees, the trees, the trees.

Fishes out of Water

Last Spring when the very crunchy ice went out under
Winnipeg's many city bridges (Osborne, Redwood and Maryland
And to the April heat skies opened wide as a staring crocus,
When we loped by the river we were aware that people eyed us—
For our moods showed up clear blunt steeples in that prairie land—
As, walking and talking, we betrayed a childish lusting for
Those wider vistas and whiter walls on the far green shore.

The city's children were racing along the banks; their filled wishes
Rushed naturally out to the brown waters and the frozen fishes
And all that tangle of jammed ice-pans and mangled dusty
Disorder come from fascinating border towns: shiny or rusty
Tin-cans, bedsprings rammed into joking bicycle
Shapes the wheels with spokes of straw and icicles,
And delicious driftwood shapes the colour of winter fishes.

Because they belonged in these waters the children shook
Off school and all dull care quicker and easier far than we can lose
Deep longings for the quiet homepool even should we choose;
But our salvation was to plumb those muddy waters with a clear look
And know how that wide, salt-drawn river took
(Just as some loving river takes longing you and me)
All that was loss and dross to the cleansing Sea.

By You It's Four O'Clock Yesterday

By you it's four o'clock yesterday:
You jump clap hands and tell
Eternal One Big Poem Time.

Outside the Snowmachine grinds, flashes
Signals proudly toward Omaha.
Nightroom Blossoms shrink back on the Vine
Stale Export smoke crawls up the walljam.

Downtown somebody will have missed the last bus:
He'll be stamping feet at the United Cigar Store
While the stars wait to guide him across town.

By you it's four o'clock yesterday:
Marking the moment that the giant
Fell asleep under the white drifts
In Sharrat's yard.

Amethysts

My grandfather once brought

a lump of rock

and then another lump of rock purple pink
each year two or three pieces of it
each year from Fort William

there sat the lumps on his hump-back trunk
beside the large uglygreen collarbox
featuring Colonel Cody (wherein were:
those lucky ten-dollar gold-piece tie-pins
that were going to my brother)

                We asked, 'And how's the Sleeping Giant?'

              'O, the Sleeping Giant
                                  still is sleeping!'

              (these jewels that were once his eyes
              have seen enough of weeping.)

this poem's made for amethysts, in that cubbyhole of mind, beside
the rather superlifelike lilacs painted by a friend

But I wonder what became of them (amethysts) in the end?

And what's become of grandpa's eyes & cheeks & bones?

And where's that little girl who spat out precious stones?

The Children and the Storm

Children before the storm ran wild—
Like pink lightning, like pink cotton dresses, came their cries—
They shrieked, they sang, they swung on the silver Hydro wires
Tussled on the yellow grass
Laughed, wrestled and scuffled
In blue jerseys showed their muscles
Turned and tied a guy to the stake: Burn up, Burn up, they chimed
Climbed into parked cars
Lifted spark plugs, shifted gears
Dug deep holes, stole for keeps
Kept tripping the girls
Who were skipping, senselessly skipping, their feverish hearts in their faces
They ran races
Were stabbed with hatred
They rollerskated like thunder down under the viaduct
Wrote on the walls with chalk
They walked the rails
Knocked over garbage pails
Rode no-handed over curbs
Read the funnies
Demanded money for the picture show
Threw stones at street-car windows
Broke bones by the dozens
Chased their brothers with clippers, nipped their cousins
Cursed cops, yelled as if they would never stop:
Startely Telystar
(and cut numerous capers selling their papers)
Jiggled and giggled
Sucked cokes, told dirty jokes
Swung rubber hoses, wiped their noses
Bruised their knees on the gravel
Travelled the baseline on the seats of their jeans
Mean and nasty, cast the following slurs on their neighbours ears:

Liar. Liar. Twenty feet higher.
Catlicker. And *O Shut Up.*
(Hearing, you would have thought they were adults.)
They railed at the radio with its static to bother
Automatically goaded their mothers
On the floor wailed: *She hit me first.*
Setting the table broke all the dishes they were able
When it came to the worst, wept and were slapped
Then the storm burst *—*
Rich kiddies were taken onto laps
Bidden a chocolate smile or a licorice one
And the rain came out like the sun.
In the slum districts those who had endeavoured
To get the toddlers in before the rain
Cleverly sent them out to wash again
Nor were the wet forgotten
Dried and free of doubts
Almost too fagged-out to eat or brag
They dragged themselves dully to bed
In woolly pyjamas they kissed their mamas
Listened to the humdrum rain overhead.

Downstairs the rugs and walls and chairs
Lolled in the small talk, stocks
And bonds, news and views,
Taxes and taxis, rackets and jackets,
A good thing for the farmers.
Will it turn warmer?

Cigarettes, smoke, anecdotes
Darning, making preserves, earning
And learning. Wasn't soandso thrilled?
How were the children?

She observes with reserve they had been pretty wearing, tearing about
Worn themselves out
The sleep of the just
It must be.
Outside the wind's fret is like a soaked summer dress on a lost child
Children after the storm are warm and mild.

Butterfly Window

She's coming out the butterfly window through
last year's filthy mosquito netting, first
one foot then the other feels for the roof

                 Slowly

She's not talking to me, she's talking
to the big Horse Chestnut latinlike
rain leaf & moss wetroof talk,

                    She's three

and hasn't gone to school where
she'll learn Canadian things like:
2 lines, 2 lines

hands on your heads everybody

and *in the basket with it*

& all those senseless things that trees don't say.

Throwing a Cigarette into Water

I like 'if not, where would I be?' I like
Ram straight back and forth from Lab Fish,
Shakuntlar straight of Amaryllis:
'We have much nicer in Bombay.'

Motown some like.
None like falling from the Reactor
None like the freshet drownings farther south.
Some gorge on Catfish, some regurgitate.

I like Water best but the rest
of the family prefer fire,
treat me like an old incendiary.

A Poem for my Professor

There is no way to tell
How you took us all Heart and Owl
Under your wing,
No song's singing, no gold hum
Can quite translate your clear story.

In the deeps of the trees certain tense dryads kept up a fluting vigilance.

The falling and fluttery birds in the dim wood
Were not those hoverers and whirrers in the aswarm air
(those were angels whose brown whicker is heard like dried keys over the asphalt)
I saw soft puffballs, little conies, I heard
Bees banging away in the brambles;
I never knew that in that sunsoaked day you who were a honey
Would soon be as out and as under as that groundhog deep in clover.

While we were lying under the terrific trees you were on your way there.

Nor had I ever realized the intense composure of brown;
Had only seen the roses dry up with wrestling a brown wind,
Had felt the hot brown chasing-after-me earth,
Had considered it all motion like green
And was puzzled how they fitted you away so nicely-
It was your cell, the brown heart seed, and it became you well.
Everything is there in the warm cell ...
The shimmering fiorenza trees, the startling blue-bell sky,

    The red cloud whence the clue clicks through ...
    O our darned awkward angel, tell us, tell us again, let us discover
    Some pencilling left behind in our but-begun philosophies.

O and before she took you, the big earth, at the last
Didn't you hear cry out Leibniz with his silver voice of alarm?
Didn't you see his minnows, minutes, hundreds to the minute, all aswim,
Before it went all shotsilk and then black and before the lights went on
And you went into that brown room?

There is no way to tell,
No song is singing, no gold hum
Equals that Timecome
And your taking off Heart and Owl
Just as you were.

It Is a Rainy Day in March

it is a rainy day in March
and my landlady is going to
another burial to-day
she will stand for an hour
with bowedhead in the small sleet
and she will weep
for her friend who died on Tuesday last
and she will cast an herb on his tomb

Goldenrod yellow by a pond

she in bright blue at his side.

it is a rainy day in March
in the year of an early Easter
she will draw close her black weeds
and she will make her small black feet march
to the cemetery side
where her husband lies
and she will look down on his many a green wreath.

Twenty kinds of clover shake the hills

she white as a stone following him.

Sea Gone Girl

The sea gone girl is all at sea
Stockings rolled below the knee,
Careless slung the dishtowel hung
Cat got its parting scatscatscat,—
For her the very breeze of a Marine
Was signal for abandoning.

The screendoor bangs, the little street
Is window-wide a-buzz with her retreat:
She makes it to the sad hotel
Is keel-hauled by the firebell pull
In lobby; then she rises to the tropic
Islands rolling home in beer and frolic.

Others have that bleached hair, part 'done'
Part rendered just uncombable by wind & sun,
Others wear fishnet gowns in this and other towns,
Have nails like Turner sunsets going down,
Knuckles that are wrinkled as a fishwife's bum,
Have voices stored in shells that make a deepsea hum.

But who else has three captive princesses
Mild-mannered, magical, wearing middy dresses?
The six-year-old has her bath drawn ready,
The seven-year-old holds the coffee-pot steady,
& the eight-year-old draws the net of her nightdress over her head
And casts the sea gone mother into bed.

The Bellringer

I ring the festive bell, Festival
celebrating dear someone's House & Life in Winnipeg;
whose sheerest happiness fiddlestrings the stairwell
(Wife, Children with the radiance of Hearth
all sing a kettleful of Joy and Mirth),

whose picturewindow slides in the gold air and shoots out green
leafy comets and jewelglints of household objects all seen
as well-cared, well-beloved under a glass of bliss.
Once in the Rijkmuseum or in some Antiquarian show
I saw sweet figures circling about a Cup like this:

when stroked it bonged out a deep hoarse note.
So if I take this Human bubble up, thimblepied it will chime whole
O Joy we're here. And then it will knell,
Entirely knowledgeable of all that's rotting
And maturing in Nature and in the nature of us all.

My Granddaughters
Are Combing Out Their Long Hair

Poem

I do not want only
The shy child with the shock of slippery wheatlike hair
Standing alone after her first communion
By the white picket fence,
She is light and airy
She is for once still and stilled her shrill voice,
She is like a beefy window curtain
Or a lacy Breughel
And must be trained in the right way
Lest she twist and turn like a very poem.
I want the others too.
I want the baby in—
He who sits under the hollyhocks
His behind the exact same shade as the Purple King hollyhock at the very top.
I want too the neighbour looking over with a leer
At the big sister got up to look like Rita Hayworth
White as white as in a restaurant.
I want the young Socialist on the corner with his cough
I want the mother
Though they tell me she lies in the churchyard
That is halfway up Montreal Mountain.
I want the man who sits on the steps of the Mayfair Washing Machine Co.
This morning and every morning
Wearing a dirty hockey sweater and holding his head in his hands.

And I too
After adjusting the focus
I shall go just as natural among them all;
Why must the lover and the sufferer be out?
I do not want the shy child only
Aloof for the one minute of her life;
I want it to be like a lacy Breughel.

The Obvious Skies

He never says what's written in the obvious skies, my father,
instead he will give you details like
they found him in a trench with 2 Germans
about the middle of the war, and
I remember how he came to me about '38 when
he was making $500 a year teaching in Cheeseville and
they wanted him to take a summer course

at that time you must remember we
were living at Aunt Bella's old place
where John put up the sign saying:
Beware of Skunks! to keep the tramps off
they were used to sleeping in the barn.
—We needed the skunks there for the rats.
I nearly fell down the well too.

Well, it wasn't so bad for those summer months
and then we went up to your grandma's;
—It wasn't so bad for John he
didn't go to school yet but I had to go
for a month and I had that same teacher you
had and she insisted I could draw and even when we
drew The Honest Indian and all I could draw was
the counter and the blankets ... you can imagine
how popular I was with the Markdale kids.

Well, what you have to do is stay close to the door
all during recess, and you were lucky that your
Aunt Marge-to-be was a big girl and the Smiths
were always kind to us; not smart but easy-going;
—I know she walked me part-way home ...

He did marry and he must have a widow somewhere;
Of course they would be Stewarts, you must
remember the farm where he grew up.
And looked up daily at the obvious skies.

White Bracelets

we all have old scars
and sometimes in winter
I can still see what was
white bracelets
(let's call them white bracelets
just as my grandmother used to say
when we fell down steep stairways,
stop crying or you'll miss hearing
the stairs—they're still dancing)
what was once white bracelets
what before that showed pink
what before that was raw & festering
what before that was agony
down to the bones
what before that was
almost blacked out
& being dragged by the tractor
in the barbed wire
what before that was
surprise & yelling:
can't you STOP   STOP
what before that was
lying in the grass
reading a blue letter
looking up into sun & clouds
that were riffed
and quiet like white bracelets.

An Afternoon's Teasing …

On a day so hot that farm dogs, cats, geese, and goats
Had had enough and lay extended, letting millers at their coats,
Clocks at their feathers, burrs and docks gnarl and gather,
Mrs Burrows was out sitting teasing up wool in the garden grass.

Under the Duchess apple tree small yellowing leaves kept falling,
Tent caterpillars kept spinning our their lavender wares, lolling
Cats on the parquet looked at Mrs Burrows larkily
Teasing out wool over the bright eyes of any birds to pass.

Abe Burrows turned in the field, rain was as certain
As his wishes, driving the tractor up, through the thick curtain
Of his thoughts it was a white girl-bride under an apple tree he caught
Sight of, not brown wrinkled Julia busily teasing wool in the grass.

Tired Abe took a long drink at the pump that quenched his vision well
But he still stood there musing when the first spears of rain fell
Ambushing Julia, who slowly gathered up her snowy teased wool,
Losing forever an old man's bearded face in the mass.

She Wore a Look of Looking

She wore a look of looking (watch she keeps)
And one day walking through the Middle Park,
Among the tall and so tapestrial trees
The three-inch spires of the churches sees;
And over all the subtle halo hung of Time.
She thought, I'd love to trace its rutted brow
And fix the dilate eye of minute ... Now ...
Instead she listened to the spire's chime,
And wore a look of looking (watch she keeps)
Scenting the twilight blossom into dark.

The Green Family

I will begin to delineate the green family.
Under the shade of the mother sat the father
small weedy and seedy
wearing his light hair daubed on his forehead;
he was a salvation army man, weekdays
he moved ashcans for the city.

His children were all mouths diligent with love of honey.
They could have spelled down anybody's child.
Sitting in the front row at the library hour
they let their darned black legs hang down,
all of them thin as water spiders, and the gold
dream of his trumpet kept them whole.

Summer sand could have held them
like five smooth stones. Off to one side
was the mother being a flowering-bush in her housedress.
They consulted about the special ride; at twilight
he took the three biggest ones aboard
that marvel of a varnished speedboat and went off in a wave.

He could not walk on water. When the shock came
he was a gallant giving his arm
in perfect faith to his three small daughters,
told them the longest story they had ever heard;
going along that hollow walk by the lake
they came to the all-gold sugar bush of the tale.

The airforce dragged
him up pale as a weed-draped Shiva;
one of the other mothers told that she was knitting
a wee red jacket for her Rita that would have been
more mere red flesh though and no sort of preserver.
Henry had been an angel.

I cannot bring my heart to mourn
his unreturn,
nor can the remnant that remember him
remembering he looked last into the sun
that was a golden gabriel and sang him home.

The Strawberry Bed: a Paradox

> Epitaph: Here lies a good wife, gentle and kind,
>   So sweet we have no fault to find:
>   What made her life so very sweet
>   Was luscious strawberries to eat.

Old Ben complained that coming-on of Spring
Meant those blood lamps would once more burn
For Carrie. That all Summer long she'd swing and watch
The crimson globules in the patch,
That when Fall brought the vine-covering rite
She'd carry on like crazy half the night
To find some cold porridge comfort in the Seed Catalogues
When Winter forced them down like two groundhogs.

Behind the yellow house that Ben had built her
Aunt Carrie had a berry bed of some pretension,
It leaped the starting gun at burnt-out twitchgrass border,
Rifled on the left flank an abstract pile of rusted things—
(Old whiffle-tree, old shares, old mattress-springs)
And fetched up at the Driving Shed in full extension.

In summer green-red-beige, that bed would hit out very hard
Against tomatoes, and the PEI potatoes whose clever Coleopteras
Were foiled by frequent dustings; at right a canny chicken-wire
Kept those bantam birds of prey at bay; while in the middle
Distance even the bottle-hung cherry-tree played second fiddle
To Berry Paradise where Carrie reigned like Cleopatra.

Afternoons while the Codling Moth sucked at the Duchess Tree,
From her wide purple panoply of a hammock Carrie's mottled feet slithered
Over the maidengrass (ugly and arty as an old walrus, she wore
Flowered prints). And o she doted on her hot-tongued treasures:
O her red-rumped legioneers, o her plump paramours! To tell her pleasures
In the berry bed would require a whole harem of angels playing zithers!
Each year when frost forced the pumpkin earlier to the Root House
And Ben pottered about, Carrie would cry out at the whirl of the seasons;
Then she would be consoled downstairs, passing in review

Canned pears, peaches, greengage plums and cherries,
Raspberries, currants, blueberries, and blackberries—
But ever sticking to her first sweet love for personal reasons.

And when her diabetic leg had her quite down
Then dear Aunt Carrie would beguile us children
To sneak her in jam tarts—my how she licked her sticky lips!
And old Ben thought he had to use his Scotch sixth sense
To trace the secret source of succulence,
But we all knew it was Forbidden Fruit that killed her.

Carrie's last suffering showed in that face
Washed of all longing, not a trace
Visible of that lascivious queen
And hot camp-follower she'd been;
Dog-tired, but as the day she was married,
Chaste was Carrie buried,
And old Ben's bones with hers did shortly twine
To guard against all inroads of that vine.

> What made her life so very sweet
> Was luscious strawberries to eat:
> Here lies a good wife, gentle, kind,
> So sweet we have no fault to find.

Blue and Yellow Boy

The little blue and yellow boy seen sitting on his mother's knee
Wore blue trousers and a light blouse,
Had a head that looked as if it had been held up
And cut under a buttercup;
He had eyes as blue as the blue roof of a house.
When he began to talk
His tongue cut and curled every last word
Like a tender dandelion stalk.
I thought out this picture
Of his future I had no doubt—
It all hung on his jagged hair and his jagged tongue.
His parents simply listened to him
And brushed his bangs back like an ordinary son.

Walk 5

A volcano recently erupting somewhere
    has freshened the evening air:
Under the streetlamps, too beautiful
to be described in plain english canadian,
    She strolls along without a care.

The odd character waiting for his bus will stare—
    'Pardon; but haven't we ... somewhere?
    Maybe over at Rahab's one evening? No??
    Maybe after the Dead Queen's funeral???'
She's sorry, but she leaves him standing there

and crosses (with green ocean in her hair)
    wondering, is he unaware
    Each streetlamp holds more faces
    than cities by the thousands?—
It's a lady in a lamp he's seen somewhere.

So André Gide was Dead

So André Gide was dead—And we
(Ilse, Lise and I) were with the leftist guy
And that sex story-teller of an Anglophile
Engaged in drinking tea.

The Red was savage with his cup
And said: All France is so divided, it must fall!
His chum scribbled away, writing of love and bicycles,
And yawned once, and once said, Drink up!

Listening to Lise and Ilse, I saw
The feminine sense for happiness, best
When they simply leave it be—A common hatred of rutabaga
Gave them a common hatred of the War.

Neither tea-leaves, I thought, nor old brown men
Can tell what crystal's holding our split light
This quiet afternoon—nor what magnetic rendez-vous
Will draw us on to meet again.

Idea for an Elegy: Finished up for the Brinks

Behind St. Peter's strolls the cinderpath
a hazy day and two nuns pass (I stand by):
One has a face like a freckled egg, Irish, and accented
I would say straight Sandwich or some border town;
the other older sallower Belgian-born from La Salette—
Joyful, their four eyes soar and won't cast down—
   'So many more gulls. So many strange gulls.
    So many strange gulls. More since the Seaway …'
when they turn off toward the grotto it is as damp
as if they had dumped the grotto down on the riverbank.
                      Five o'clock
is calling the lost hours home:
Fly back! calls Middlesex
Right now! calls St. Peter's
Bell towers take the time from glint of wings
clear up the Thames. My wheels are still silver
on the cinderpath … those gulls *are* abundant, beady eyes
that have taken in Detroit, insouciance of Montreal;
multitudes of gulls, freckled, fresh-starched,
travel creased or whatever
   (So many strange gulls. Up from the Seaway.)
                       take up a sad calling:
Of Sylvia Plath. O Sylvia Plath.

Aristide Bruant au Honey Dew

Deep in Lautrec's lovely eyes
Struggles the surge of violent seas;
Well-bred ladydogs sniffing the Musakladen airs
Put him at unease.

It is an hour of tea; furs
Unfold their brown orchids in the smoke;
From each sweet claw dangles the little dagger
Too indolent for stroke.

Waitresses wear their cup-coloured clothing
To conceal a violence like artificial hydrangeas;
Eyes that should have been running rivers into lakes together
Pass as desert strangers.

O for Bruant to come blasphemous, talking up ready storms,
Raging to give the waiting girls their cue
To come forth all clatter and vile orange welcome, and to put
An absinthe in each Honey Dew.

Getting the High Bush Cranberries

    I looked up suddenly and the sky
    was full of them, sky
    was on fire with them.

    Following her directions I find
    the purple maple
    walk the mosslog
    deeper into the bush
    veer at the rushes
    test for sinkholes
    crawl the rabbitdropping undergrowth
    straighten up
    and the sky is full of them, sky
    is on fire with them.

(got the fence up here
a long story
so it's beginning
to look like Story Book Farm
after all
after a lot of work
also we've been laying in
crab-apple jelly
wild-grape jam
wild-cranberry & the like
and Arthur was into the chokecherries
for the wine also
I brandied some wild-plums
which I will never do again
as you have to pierce each
dratted little plum
with a needle
it's so nice to be settled in
Do come & see us)

The Lake is directly in front of me but
High Bush Cranberries swaying muddle up
locations: dis
mayme   dis
turbme   dis
locate

years of the instinctive glance
for bears over the shoulder
I begin picking, shouting
out to Burning Lake:

This is only Watergate Year
It's not Year Whole World on Fire
Not that Year yet.

My Granddaughters Are Combing Out Their Long Hair

my granddaughters are combing out their long hair sitting at night
on the rocks in Venezuela   they have watched their babes
falling like white birds from the last of the treetop cradles
they have buried them in their hearts where they will never forget
to keep on singing them the old songs

brought down to earth they use twigs, flint scrapers acadian
their laughter underground makes the thyme flower in darkness

my granddaughters are thin as fishbones & hornfooted but they are
always beautiful under the stars: like little asian paperthings
they seem to open outward into their own waterbowl

mornings they waken to Light's chink ricocheting
off an old Black's Harbour sardinecan.

Reduce them the last evangelines make them part of the stars.

my granddaughters are coming out by night combing their burr
coloured hair by the rocks and streamtrickle in Venezuela
they are burnt out as falling stars but they laugh
and keep on singing them the old songs.

Lullaby of the Child for the Mother

The child who never lived was the real child
whose lovely eyes were seas
and little limbs were lullabies
and lovely seas

He said, my mother is a street
where strangers pass
her hair winds like the wind
round wooden poles

Her lovely eyes are seas
Her hair is wind that shakes the elder tree

He said, my mother is a stair
where strangers pass
and when night rocks me round
then I am sure
Her hair is wind that shakes the elder tree
her eyes are seas

Sunday Morning

To the deepboom of bells and the conch, steeple
tolling down, heart-tug of traffic on the Bay highway
the cannonade on the not-too-distant front,
sounds of the officer's horse muffled by snow—
to Sunday morning waken.

(the officer sees that this one is supporting that one somehow
Robinson answering for Robinson,
the surgeon sees through his white scarf just as clearly
as the Viking helmsman scans the fog)

Sunday morning: whistle the coffeepot awake.
Hard leaves are whirling at the windows.
Piles of the week-end papers colour up the rug.

But the deepboom of bells and the conch, hooves
of the officer's horse muffled by snow ... sounds
torn out of me waking bind me to the lost inland words
that answer week of days, eastwall, westwall,
the fogbound longships jesting at it all
and the lost Robinsons endlessly standing Roll Call.

'It Is As If They Were Never There'

It is as if they were never there.
The wildflag tumbled off the windowsill
witches looking in
the children turn themselves small
& climb into the coffeepot to hide.
Words can conjure up buffalo thunder
westwind west wind west, my brother sings
& tosses his brightest pennies against the luckless sky.

There does exist somewhere
a little island that seems to be a desert:
Paul said he would claim it
& took the family there, the smallest child found
one root of one tree peculiar
sand particles glistening on the rootlets;

That sand led them to find the springhead
drilling through volcanics that's easy
a few weeks   a few ballpoint pens later
the hillside trickle moved down the slope
and fetched up at an eternity of dunes;

They buried plover eggs   scratched off small shellfish
harvested various kelp for various uses,
and in the burrow
weeks at a time they dreamed out
clover bees and tiny cowbell sounds
while trackers on the dunes blistered & bitter
walking over them searching their traces
abandoned, concluding they were never there.

Protectiveness

You are always getting lost in a hundred ways:
out raspberry picking you wander in the worst places
for bears, why? And why when the boat founders do
they all jump out but you? And what about the time
we were haying?

We were haying on a very steep hill beside a lake.
The wagon went on and I went more slowly looking for
gentians. I heard the noise dimly or felt some shock
but I knew: they've tipped into the lake. Too many
on the load. Exactly what they'd do.

I raced down the hillside and followed the track by
the lake. A rather steep bank. At the fence-angle
there was the slightest wooden bridge to be crossed,
hardly over the water but over the treacherous edge
of the drainage ditch, reeds where the ducks nested.
A large culvert emptied there. And this was where
the load had tipped. It was slanted half under,
precariously. Heads, hands, legs were bobbing about.
Even as I clambered gingerly out on the stones to
give a hand, all the while calling your name and
asking, even then the great shock necks of the horses
were dipping away, unharnessed. The front end of the wagon
(and you were the driver) heaved and began to disappear.

All the while calling your name I gave a hand to those
I could help from the load. I pulled out your father,
your mother. I pulled out by their wet green hands
my father & my mother. I prodded down arms length
into the hay and pulled out your grandfather and your
grandmother. And my grandpa and my grandma their hair
bewildered and quite stiff from fright. All the while
calling your name, inquiring and asking, I sifted that
wispy, floating-off-farther hay, and I kept on stretching
my arms down and down and down. And then when I had
pulled at longlast from deep in the mud, and cleaned it

from his beard and face, your great-great-grandfather,
and hauled him more dead than alive to the bankside,
I saw with despair that the wagon had pitched under.
There were no more then on the load.

While I was weeping, the rescued imbeciles on the green bank
thought only of wringing out their shirt-tails. When I stopped
asking them what we should be doing and turned to look for some
ripple or clue on the blue lake, they walked away over the hill
together. They walked round to the opposite bank straight
into the sun. And then suddenly they waded in toward me,
disappearing and dissolving like the silver links of a chain.
Crazily still calling your name, I broke out part of the logs
of the bridge and built on the spot a raft and took a long
fencerail for a pole. I thought I would pole along and
check the likeliest spots on the bottom. I went slowly
and warily along the sun's one path of silver, thinking
you may have floated, injured, off the front part of the load
and be caught here somewhere.

I poled rapidly over the lake's blue top seeing the very place
on the hill where the gentians grew. Looking down, letting
your name fall clear as a bell circling down. Places I could
see bottom. It was strewn with buttercups daisies gentians
clover. Here and there, as though aimlessly gleaned,
floated forkfuls of hay. But you were not there.

I beached the clumsy raft. In desperation I jumped onto the
top of the rack, tipped but not quite yet underwater and there
I felt the force of the water rushing back into the culvert.
I wondered whether you had been sucked through there. There
was muck at the entrance but enough water to dive in.
The culvert grew narrow a little partly cobbled between cement
where I touched frogcoated and fusty. Twigs, grass, winter
food for the muskrats had been dragged in. I wondered whether
I would meet the chain of ancestors and how to get out then.

Then breathing got terribly easy. I came into a circle of
light out of the muck and into a reedy place where the ducks had been.

The reeds there still bore the imprints of their many soft
bodies. What water there was had been cuddled quiet into
a dull sort of peace. I thought, I can't go on any farther.
I will stay here and rest and be rocked. For somewhere, I
thought, somebody else must be looking after you.

I Have Confused the Feeling

I have confused the feeling
Though should know as right as rain
That from this slowtrain window I have seen
A previous pass of plain;

Unquiet as hair of nib or the poised drill,
And does no good to strain
The landskip countenance to divine
What the unreasoning season won't explain—
What eyes looked asters into mine.

As though they'd laid a pleasing anxious hand on time
And made it spin
Till where I'd been and whither to have gone
One in the whirling one in the wheeling
Iron of the sun;

I have confused the feeling
Though should know as right as rain
That from this slowtrain window I have been
In that slowpassing plain.

Neruda Walks In

Neruda walks in over the airwaves.
Later Broughdale will go back to being Broughdale.
Now he's walking our streets.

girls in shawls send up the fallen leaves
to gyro round him,
the Fisher twins ride through him
two on a bike

Dogs & Cats though sense a bristle of difference.
The Four Winds rush to whirl his words away
and it's an ordinary street again, an ordinary day.

The Brown Family

All round the Browns stretched forty acres of potatoes.
They lived like squatters in my father's little chicken-house
That grew to lean-tos and then to a whole shack-town where married Browns
Slept God-knows-how hilled in the darkness all night long,
Mornings how rolled out to breakfast on the lawn
Sitting in crumbs and clover, their eyes still glozed over
With dufferish sleep, and all stuffing away like Eskimos.

Brown boys had greasy jeans and oilcloth school-bags made at home
And sneakers for quick escapes through orchard gates,
Tom had two left thumbs while Ted was tough and dumb, but there was much
Of army sadness to the way all their heads got furry as muskrats by March.
Well after meagre spells Fall was their full season when they dropped
Partridge, pheasant and squirrel—shooting as if they would never stop
As later they crazily shot up even the apple trees at Caen.

Their sisters inevitably called Nellie or Lily were deliberately pale,
Silly incestuous little flirts whose frilly skirts were dirty
From every ditch in the county. On lonely country roads under the moon
Their sadness lit like incense their sweet ten-cent perfume.
But at hint of insult their cheeks took on fiery tints those summers
When they hired-out to cook. And their eyes often had that strange blue look
Of the blue willow plates round a rich farmer's plate-rail.

'What I can touch and take up in these two hands,' said Mrs Brown,
'Is what I trust!' Accordingly on the bashed piano and on the floor, dust
And rich potato-coloured light everywhere mingled: scraps, fronds, gourds,
Teazle, fossils, hazel wands, turkey feathers and furs ... goods
All lovingly hers tangled. And all could be taken up, stroked, cajoled
In the same manner as her Old Man: for Mr Brown's heart was pure glossy gold
By tender handling, of all that's drossy, slowly, suvendibly, rendered down.

But as alike as Anna Pauker's brood so that it tears the heart to see
Was that last lot and will all Browns ever be,
Picking and pecking at life, scratching where something is cached.
What are they looking for? Not lots to eat or wear. Not lots in town.
Strangely, that same thing *we* want would satisfy a Brown—
Something of the sort God gives us every day
Something we can take up in our two hands and bear away.

Walk 4

Up all birds and absolutely
shred the unclove air above this sampler yard
whose edges are acacia, pine, bluebush and elm hedge;

Cry silence at the childish *arrangements of jumps*
that are ever-ending in a sprawl of leotards
uplofting, the red and black ones of that centaur age;

And just forgive their mother out raking leaves and saying
martha with her left hand mary with her right, pulling hard
right into winter with her autumn rage.

O send down purer light upon these dear embroiderings
till we can see the wanderers by White Dahlia Walk;
Rimbaud in surcoat, dear Mike Todd, lean on the sundial to talk,
when all is all-illumined with these wings.

King's Park, Manitoba

north: Mrs Roker's raking

Look! Mrs Roker's raking up Time:
when the last leaves fall it's sad as all Valhalla
there's Mrs Roker raking up Time

    in a man's suitcoat
    in a grim poke
    by her pokerfaced house
    with its squarechip eyes
    there's Mrs Roker raking up Time

then o so slow old river leaves green trees near bend
winds winds on still   till Spring Summer Fall all pass
o turn o see all gone   o bare clay banks there   o sparse
dark grass where once passed buffalo buffalo buffaloes
in broad-shouldered big gang pressed passed
so people ran indoors in ran ran till crush press pass
big tan scurfy herd all gone gone gone

    in a man's suitcoat
    in a grim poke
    by her pokerfaced house
    with its squarechip eyes
    there's Mrs Roker raking up Time.

west: Perera's Yard

Under a bloated moon they are digging in Perera's Yard
ripping the sundayparlourgrass close to the raspberry bed.

Charleyjack is goddamning the gumbo; his little purple dog
whines on the rope by the polelight wants to come & dig.

—Always the quiet one, always just sit there
the Old Lady rubs at the stain on the stairs.

wheezing bentover bentunder the Old Man is shouldering him in
—This here is the House Of The World, Charliejack as usual sings.

   o but that briar, o but that root
   that's my own life goes into the snakewood
   and it's my lot too
                         bopped by a bottle
dumb and left lying out there in Perera's Yard.

south: Ukrainian Wedding of the Canned Vegetables

The Canchucks chockful cupboards are in an uproar
it's the first wedding for this year

> now sealers in the cellar we've
> at last heard the Canchucks leave
> off for some country wedding o the horns the yells
> for whiskey cash & pretty girls;
> now we're alone at last don't loiter
> come dance at the wedding of my daughter.

Glowing like an old beet in the dawn
with goodwill is the bride's father (a quart of borscht)
he holds fast Mama's hand (a sunwashed flaxen cob of corn)
presenting proudly on the other side
a radiant Gem Jar of a bride
(o succulent yellowtop that fall mushroom)
she stands beside her pickled onion groom.

> o concentrated small are happy happy acres there
> full amplified in every jar
> o golden sum of gardens, breezes move
> and undulate a ferny grove

> while calm she muses on her love

> all in a wondrous ring
> gay interlacing carrots sing
> o so sweet so very sweet 'tis
> our felicity and your bliss

So circle round her now and sing her female cousins:
peas, corn, mixed veg. there by dozens
all merry, all bright. Only one old Miss Dill ('68)
sniffs: Young people nowadays can't wait.
then the groom's father firm on his chickenlegs
raps silence for a toast seriously begs:

    Friends our garden days are done
    but ever in our hearts may shine the Sun
    sweetening our days the whole bleak winter long.

Then come the drinks, the kissing, the wishes
for long happiness and fruitful lives
trays whirl by   the long table loses dishes
of western dainties and the cashpile thrives
quite abandoned tomatoes dance heads thrown back
madly about the room collide
a roué uncle Pickle runs amok
and wrests the shoes right off the bride.

              *

ah but they'll fade away   merry now until the dawn
& then they'll hear the Canchuks come
& then they'll neatly glide
bride & bridegroom sidebyside
to face sure winter hastening on.

east: Timesend's Grove

>in the green oakgrove at Timesend's
>is blowing a pink rose special to that shade:
>peculiar, wild and soft, not lasting, it has affinity
>with what my Dolphin Baby said to me:
>*We're all aswim in one big sea*

out lying on the green grass beside the hedge and under the scrub
oak trees, I was watching two children coming through the dust
knee-high (and the bees were about and were zooming after those
yellow warblers that go lacing through the hedge) and with never
a sign they drifted over to the grove and snitched each one a whole
banner of roses that they held close to their jerseys till they were
nearly out of sight when suddenly they loosened up and began
madly swinging roses. Then only the mid-day left very hot
and I was listening to the wash-wash voice of my baby who was asleep
and who suddenly said, We're all aswim in one big sea.

>O Joy, the lightest tap can stir a failing sun
>can give the labouring globe a spin
>that starts a staggering miraculous run
>of roses, trees and we and we
>who do all swim in one big sea.

As If In Code ...

It's worse over the mountains.
Jettison this and that
dance round the fires till dawn
throws a light lasso
and draws the flatlands in;
Jettison this and that
till point grows into dash
and we get pushed on
by the biggest star in the world.

Unmapped the Blue Mountains.

But everyone goes over anyway
way up and over into that long passage
of no colour but cold, looking back
at the crazed fires blazing on the plains:
chuckle of longlugged books, carvings, embroidery,
fires make the past a garden of glads;
roar of dishes, tablecloths, chain bracelets
getting gay as mountain lions or cougars;
swish of baptismal bonnets and winding-sheets
flick round the site like brookfish;
'... one day see I just happened to be going along Piccadilly St ...'
'... once I saw I forget but it was light ...'
fast and free all things with wings.

Fire out. All fires nearly out now.
Seawinds smooth the hands that are crags now
Vineleaves bud on the rawhide circling the brow.

In Leningrad ...

In Leningrad the truck delivering bread slewed
and stalled in the snow and spilled out
loaves that the passersby picked up
and put back   I read

and Gladys tells us laughing behind her eyes
how it was so bad when they came down from Schreiber
and couldn't get used to the eastend and Punch
stole and others stole:

(they called it swiping then)

<u>one case eggs</u> (that's 288 eggs we had
eggs coming out of our ears from
Humes Transport, Windsor-Toronto,
they could spare it)

<u>one case cornflakes</u>, (that's a dozen
boxes off the line at Kellogg's)
<u>one case perfume</u> (cleaning old Duncan's
basement, not getting paid anyway)

and that's nothing, when they switched at Schreiber,
we used to pry the lids off the cars and take a
couple of cases of whiskey they had to fire
the whole night gang, the CPR

In Leningrad that winter it had passed
the point where you would be shot for stealing
bread, but the difference between being poor
and being starved also passes just as night & day.

A Shame

Here in the Aggie Macphail country where
children take turns coming to school
saving the shoes and choring
Angels in Quebec have sent in the snowmobile
Angels in Georgia have opened up Beaver Valley
they are making trails in Eugenia
and there will be cartocar from Mexico soon
to the Devil's Glen
Angels in NYC will make paradise in Feversham
where the Guernseys are going.

With the right kind of nights
and sun on the snow
in February or March the last stand of maples
say ready;
we will haul the old woodburner out of the sugar shanty
all the children will stay home to help
wearing their boots from Poland
and we'll get the last of the syrup;

Syrup gets used up fast you can't keep it around
and it's free for the asking or giving
poor things in the cities they never get the real thing,
and on that farm where my grandmother picked stones
while the little ones kept the kiln going
my great-grandfather died saying in Gaelic:
You're wearing the wrong tartan all of you ours is

Stewarts are buried here and there
Auckland and Pretoria, lots out near Kindersley
whence they walked back and forth to Saint John
seeing the country free for the going
time to travel during the dust-growing years.

It's nothing to give up and move on
Nothing to die that could happen to the best of us
But to die without finishing the sentence
Great-grandfather that was a waste of breath.

Song: Six Makes The Set

Six makes the set collectors
say and pin them up like fingers
won't be twisting them again;

Bashed back from Pretoria on a red
uniform left stashed where chamberpots
& Elsie Dinsmore waits;

They're glinting, they're winking back
tears for blue-eyed soldiers on duty
again they're weighing down serapes & Indian

blankets, stars in the skies, gemstones
leaping out of rivers, children dancing reels—
everything's coming in sixes.

Six makes the set.

The Rose Family

Nursing mothers may not get to mass
And in the Rose family this was the case:
Through a peephole he'd made with a hot coin
Small Blanche, Denise, Louis followed their father's going
While lulled and muddled their mother sat
Close to the full-blown stove with Marie in her lap.

What happened then? She'd tell of little Jesus so
Cruelly dead out under the snow,
Of good St. Joseph, then what they could understand
Of why the Métis girl ran off with the Big Cat-Tractor man …
Lulled and muddled, how were they to explain
That mother and rosy stove were suddenly gone

To Louis who found them crying hard
Small Blanche, Denise, Louis out in the pitted yard.
Nor when the C.N.R. rushed past
Could travellers peering through the frost
Comprehend Louis' figure, kneeling, dumb
With the three lost children crooked in his arm.

Little Pasternak Poem Promised to Mrs Neville

She has not cared in the same way since Pasternak died.
The little children snuggle at her side
And toss their yellow heads and play about the room
And stab their sunshine deep into the gloom.

As if the great familiar tree that Rilke put outside the door
Dropped a last cone and then was seen no more.
Or Verna laughed and loosened her bright ring
And let it go forever in the spring.

O invincible summer's gone! That lion head
Shocked into silver, is he dead?

Did he go down in sorrow and in doubt
As candleflame on snowy pane went out?

February 20th

The day before yesterday
my daughter and a friend
decided to put a curse on the neighbourhood boy,
they made a mudball with extra gravel
from the cemetery, welded in burdock,
blackberry thorn and the wing
of a moulty bird,
   they threw
it into a willow tangle on the creekbank.
Yesterday the neighbour boy
limped going to school as if he
had fallen off his bike or got
checked too hard at hockey;

this morning he came the two miles home
from school at 11 a.m.
kicking a stone and expecting a licking.
They got their sweaters full of stickticks
and their hair full of burrs
and their faces full of scratches
finding that mudball,
which dissolved in the creek and the feather
babbled off to the sewer, and like tears
over a body cold creek waters
kept laving the mudball.

This Iron

This iron seems to know its way:
Collar & Inside, Back, Fronts & Sleeves
it's all too easy though
                    and the sweetgrass smell
rising from the cotton takes me
                    to that tall red house
and the Sun bringing in sharp spurts
                    of melting icicles.
Collar & Inside, Back, Fronts & Sleeves
                    and Big Tear River
that Iron and Homesick One are swimming in

          & now it's that Farmhouse windbound
where the irons wait lined on the stove
and get snapped up in their handles
and slapped at those shirts
viciously reddening:
Collar & Inside
Back, Fronts & Sleeves   men,men,men.

Poem

A feeling of nightfall having been alone all day
May come by even five p.m. I put on scarves, gay gloves, leave them—
Papers, tomatoes, Morley Callaghan, the pictures (little clay
Chicken, Flower Vendor, the static redlegged horse)
Blessing what holds them in their course while I'm away.

Once in the tipsy shrug of a street I could cry aloud
Of something that tugs and bunts me against people and storefronts—
O to mash into piles of oranges, piles of pink Telys, into the crowd,
Combatting colour with a deep but china cheep, a Buy Come Buy, a redlegged neigh—
To leap with such inaudible clamour is always glamourous and proud.

Big Trees

Our backyard is beautiful to-night:
I could replant every tree
put it into its proper saucer of snow:
mr by mrs / great-uncle by great-aunt;

I light out from an old photo, cross careless
before paving days into *your* yard,
where winds are rocking a hammock,
wintertime moonlight & twigs,

(broom & unbuckle) and in handknit stockings from Ireland
now I'm skating icicletoed on the kitchen lino
past the black & silver kitchen stove
    —just let it blast my middle—till

I see *her,* graybrown tree of the past,
rocking with her crochetflowers laid in rows,
and I see *him,* flannel shirt, grey sweatercoat,
newspaper & Bible, glasses there at hand.

            *

you know, I was so small then, I let
your winds & waters rock me round
and couldn't talk enough to tell you
—Big Trees, I *like* to be with you to-night.

Spring Poem

HEARING: hearing: hearing:
The Engine warming up: warming
And the Earthworm going zupzupzup through the brown ground
Chased by that same hot crank.
Through the tunnelled air trundle the marvellous merry birds:
All carrying rich pokes, wearing super stoles
And showing off the fine detail of freckles on their tails; just as clearly
As the big block: the elephant block: the big F.
Of my mammoth city shows its grim windows and dopey blinds.

O the Engine: the Elevator: of me and mind:
It goes down its stretchy rubber cables:
Capable or incapable:
But going zupzupzup.

I had the window open

I had
the window open, giving
my Matisse
a good shaking,

when, suddenly (from the l.h. corner
near the frame) a golden gourd
throstled into a yellow bird
and was nabbed by my cat.

I was aghast
lest there be a space,
but my smallest child's smallest hand
fitted the place;

and now I have this golden girl
under a canopy of mandolins
and bottle shapes, seriously
playing out her very shady role.

Walk 3

Hand in hand we walked all round
    The world at the Equator:
Very little we saw, he
Was too busy watching out for me
And I was too busy watching the way—
    Silly because you can't go astray
    Simply following the Equator.

        *

And who did we meet, walking all round
    The world at the Equator?
Some rather recognizable faces
Tho' connected with other times, other places,
    We nodded but made a moue of doubt—
    It seemed the whole world was out
    All walking round the Equator.

        *

We grew old, of course we grew old,
But all of it has been told and retold:
All the Problems solved—how to count the many
Steps in a day, how to walk over any
Sea, how to get back to the start-
    ing point with a whole heart,
    Just how to walk round the Equator.

        *

No wonder we were often weary of walking round
    The world at the Equator.
    But it was something to do.
We thought, someday when it's all through
And people ask, we can say:
    Well, it's the well-travelled any-old way
    Following round the Equator.

Notes on a Day

Came back from searching dental periodicals
in the Russian translated into German stacks,
Office was feathered over with soft acquisitions
and Our Boss was pondering the Great Seal prior
to attack on new Books. I asked for a change of task.
'Four o'clock. Not a good time to start fresh.
Try Boston. Try the French ...'
Suddenly Margaret, at her desk, looking no different
said, 'Tether: end of.' No word more,
passed solitary angel out the gothic door.

Well, yes. Go up: go down. Try Boston. Work to rule.
Came back from searching dental periodicals
in the Russian translated into German stacks.
Our Boss cooed 'Migraine weather'
put away till tomorrow the Great Seal.
Going home I passed through Chinatown
and bought one of those pink folded-up flowers
that once in water pulses like a throat,
then skipped to ailing Maggie's doorstep, Whistled
something delightful to the tune of:
'And particularly delightful is the story of the little old
man who rode all over Moscow free because
no one could change his hundred rouble note.'

Poem

There's a waterfall in Iceland
that cries by the thousandsful,
even on a postcard it's forever saying,
don't fear again, horseman, ride on,
I'll do the crying for you.

Mr Kopf burnt off his wintergrass
it was exciting when the wind changed
and he had to phone up his brother-in-law;
for a day or so it showed black
now you can't see it for the new growth.

Saturday morning riders shyed away
from my pampas grass going up.
We all like fires and we all like waterfalls
and the brown days when gulls chase unseen
excitement over the fields.

The Barbara Suite

On Little Hecla
we washed our paisley bedspreads off the docks
and saw small trails of colour
settling down like lilies.

Those selling fish or blueberries
appeared politely at the screen-door—
Like one summer merging into another
they passed silent from porch to kitchen and away.

The lambs, afraid to jump, clung
to mother and rock. 'They don't urge them,'
said my mother. At summer's end
the lambs were all jumping.

In the store—they were so clean and clear
all the Icelanders—and yet now
I see them fuzzy, as if I
were looking through a smudged lantern.

Once, rowing to another island, I looked back
on Little Hecla and saw it shrink
—go smaller than drop from blade of oar
and merge into my own growing.

Aroha's Fossil

Aroha's fossil goes clear through the washing cycle
still in the pocket of her wrangler jeans
and comes out deepsea clean & pure as
someone's eyes are seas who's
fallen right through the world
(straight through to China as we used to say)

Keelhauling, gutting, name it—
nothing of that shows.

She says, hey here's my fossil back and
warms it in her hand.

This Elastic Moment

Yes we are that too: we are everything who feel it.
Everything that has meaning has the same meaning as angels: these
hoverers and whirrers: occupied with us.
Men may be in the parkgrass sleeping: or be he who sits in his
shirtsleeves every blessed Sunday: rasping away at his child who
is catching some sunshine: from the sticky cloud hanging over the
Laura Secord factory: and teetering on the pales of the green
iron fence: higher up than the briary bushes.
I pass and make no sound: but the silver and whirr of my bicycle
going round: but must see them who don't see: get their fit, man
and child: let this elastic moment stretch out in me: till that
point where they are inside and invisible.
It is not to afterward eat a candy: picket that factory: nor to
go by again and see that rickety child on the fence.
When the band of the moment breaks there will come angelic
recurrence.

Ten Letters

Letter One

Nobody knows where I'm buried.

And nobody knows whether our experience levers really human experience?

So fall back on somebody else with a heart sweet and easily readable:

Someone in a picture, for instance, wearing turn of the century Liberty Lawn fading to lavender,

> hair pinned in a quick bun
> she is always on that balcony
>
> overlooking the harbour
> it is always morning
> and she is always saying goodbye
>
> very tenderly and slowly
>
> to someone who is up early
> and tending a sail toward daybreak.

Is this what I mean by experience levering? Should I run up a little superstructure of sorts?

But then Ariadne was plumper, wasn't she?
Penelope marthaing away on her shuttle?
Mrs Polyphemus too bent on her kettle of plantain
eye-plasters and little leech garden?
Dido too weepy in her leopard skin?

*

Some of these days they'll be handing out sheet metal
handkerchiefs!

That's not the ending though:
I want her on my tombstone waving at the waves.

Letter Two

Really first letter to second seeing of great light

And knowledge that first light deserves telling of:

   So, Light Number 1: Letter to:

   Time: Perhaps
                noscene
                horizontals

Then so many windows opening suddenly, horizontals, verticals quite put by, and I'll be living in a palace made of light.

   Houses have walls

      to slipknot out,

      papershades, partitions,

         hard to describe except 'undecorating', but

The feeling that I'm going to be awake all day

And somebody else will be awake all day too.

Letter Three

Numbers:

The numbers of tiny rings in labelled sacks and the packets
Of very worn shoes on the plain wood shelves in plain
        numbered shacks
And the numbers blotting out the scratched names over bunks
The simplicity so great that it almost looks like a lack of imagination
Of the numbers of headstones there must (despite Mexico) be—
The numbers of very small feet that are marching forever over
the seas from China—

All these might tend to set us against numbers.

But then there are people like Marianne Moore's mother

Who say look at the stars   leaves on the aspen   grasses and grasses, fields of grass,

Look into the undepthed smiles of the levering dead.

Letter Four

Just as those long gone parcels of suffering dear Chinese poets

    in exile

Seem unable to lift the lumpy brush without:

    wine
    or a song
    or their boy

Thinking of things like:

    the South Mountain Rd.
    and/or the low green valley and the footbridge
    over which someone might just be coming ...

So must I record while thinking about how we are all exiles during
exactly 110 minutes of interruptions varied and semi-tortuous,
I have consumed

    2 stale pieces second son birthday cake
    1 cup instant coffee

And given charitable offerings to gulls with aid of small hands

And I have done motherly duties reading about St Swithin's Day
And bunking down various recalcitrants to the umpteenth.

All the while thinking on harp-like themes:

    The impossibility of you coming over the Bay
    under this exceptional sky that has been all day
    a jostle of cloud lumps like majestic hand and when I bowed just
    let one ray of glory be.

Letter Five

Gone like dreams

all the times I have trees lain under gone like dreams.

Only the absurd ones stick and tickle:

> i.e. Those friends gonetoEngland coming a crumpled way
> over a spitball landscape (pages torn from Collins'
> Ode to Evening) hubby wearing 'his own' tartan
>
> wee wifie all swathed in wool lace …
>
> best of all wifie says comfily,
>
> 'ah but they're millends'
>
> mill lends?
>
> ah mill ends!
> ah how the ends mill where the mills end,
> where Collins' Ode to Evening
> ends the miles where the Great Mill smiles.

And now all dreams all friends with glory-auriole,

> smart in the brief oriole season,

Then off to the Great Mill smiling far beyond reason.

Letter Six

All the things my mother told me seen as Eskimo carvings

In two lines facing: O that upright one brandishing a heart

      like a spear,

Ah that supplicant one holding in a heart that looks out of

      wondering eyes;

And both lines like days to be taken up in the hand

Just fondled, dandled, handled, day after day after day.

But The Somme, The Somme: could we ever live days enough

      to give it enough holding?

Even when sitting alone in darkness, quietly waiting

      out the winter?

Not alone: there's that Trinity: Time, Patience, Eternity

      many bells gently ringing.

Goethe says: Life is for living. But what is living?

Ah that upright one fists to the sky.

Letter Seven

Grandmother writes that the old square piano has been
        moved up
Up up and over the bannisters by some spring surge
Of black jackets saying let's with the old heaveho
Up and to repose in the back room:

   'Manhandle it as high
   Above the sea of city
   As tables of the law ...'

In this case piano, Pasternak, way above the seacrest
of elms, crows, old binders and rakes, the bleached
beached bones of January by the barnbank;

Away up there it will serve as tabletop
To books and candlesticks and droughty plants
A winter epic long-planned, the move up;
And somewhere another Winter's planning how the
        house crash down

Letter Eight

Place was that piece of ground between house and swing,
yielding to the foot,
covered with reddened strawberry leaves
and that small vine that isn't wintergreen.

Among the cedars, some of them struggling still like old limbo dancers,

covered with a lighter green lichen,

there on the day that William Faulkner died I came and stood
and even if I had not willed it so, down my head would have gone down,

thinking definitely about something:
God, how I love this little part of ground.

Letter Nine

Two groups or groves: These Chinese pictures! Look & see!

First one has five trees (maybe palms who knows):

Mrs B., Mr B., and three boys.

Sometimes says Mrs B. I say let's get the hell out of here

build a boat in the basement and come spring simply
        load them all
in, sail away, sail away, where? anywhere out of here. One
thing'll holdem down—fear of sharks.

Out of the portholes all sorts of creepers, vines, stretching-out
ivies from number one son's collections. All sorts of hamsters,
turtles, little fishes, hamburgers and baseball bats running
round the decks. All sorts of plague flags thumbing noses …
Dear Bs, dear Noahs, take this as Sailing Orders from our shore.

Second one is, let's see, just one (poor little poplar tree).
In Marilyn's house all the Mexican furniture being
away for finishing, oiling, recovering,
all the rugs, all the plants, all the pictures,

all the things that weren't there yet,
because she loved them, will be always there.

Letter Ten

No one knows where I'm buried but it's a happy part of ground:
After quite a long time down I go the shortcut through the Field
and I focus on one grassblade getting round a puddle
then on a browned-out square that still has lots of life
Chicory, Q. Anne's Lace, Clover.

All I can think of is why it's happening again!
And Harold Town may your eyes stay green
and keep looking at brown squares and Everlasting Stucco
and keep crawling over your own bit of happy ground.

The Martha Landscapes

The Glass Cupboard

Lights from the Highway sparser, softer now
and the Gorst lights gone and their house gone
away, just lost rib to new life in dark seas,
just dark seven sleepers gone seasabout the foot of our hill,
just the foot of the hill and a great cave opening up.

Lights from the glass cupboard !spark! the house dark;
And it's up to the glass cupboard now! It looms
at James' headheight, three paces from kitchen sink,
one from table, length approximately my armspan, crafted
by an Albertan who loved the bush, the hills.

The Bay Highway kindles to blue Italian grotto glasses;
and green glasses, safe-and-wide as Sweden; and cheap
little ruby liqueurs sing; and cocktail Libbys supermart
violent and fresh from fists that swung axes, pounded down a territory
and rolled Malcolm Lowry into the soundmad surf dazzling no warning ...

By an Albertan who loved the bush, the hills,
who made this cupboard ark that tends the tides
of dream. *They light, they guard* the house,
glow like an icon of Mike Todd, thirty-odd glasses,
touched off by random headlights moving toward the Bay.

Last Night I Dreamed

Last night I dreamed about you all under the Star Over the House Quilt;
I remember mother making it: the little squares of jonquil window lit
The doors, shutters often green. Your block has still the hollyhock (french knots)
Mine has the lilac (front yard), looking hard the lilacs still are blooming there,
The real ones down—time and town development don't affect the quilt.

Each of us, house body, and the star, the star-filled head;
Each of us bedded down lifetime dreams the star-filled town
Waking goes walking the houses of our own making, talking the blocks away.
I might move into you taking on hollyhock   but it's not
Me really just the dreaming of the star-filled head.

The Star Over the House Quilt she made it extra size;
Her eyes puzzled out each stitch; she declared her fingers to be all pricked
And she licked the blood from roofs, sidewalks, from the small yards
With the ever-blooming trees pointing to the stars
Of the Star Over the House Quilt.

My Grandmother's Sugar Shell, Ontario Baroque

My grandmother's sugar shell (spoon), Ontario Baroque, has just fallen
out of the uncleaned silver bag.
What does it mean, I wonder.
One day only I saw her stop work.
We lay out on the grass by the highway under the big maple
and two cars went by toward Owen Sound. When she heard
their car coming for dinner, she got up, a big woman
with Scottish shoulders, built too heavy on the top like
all the Stewarts, her leg-bones stilt-like in proportion
to the square rest of her.
                          And she rose all of a piece,
I remember that she rose up somehow straight and not
hinging her knees, nor using her hands, nor her elbows,
nor leaning her head forward. So that
she was the reverse of a tree falling before a quick gust.
That is, she rose on a slant as if pulleys were attached
to her everywhere   or as if
the kitchen woodstove were a magnet that suddenly
drew her inside. One minute she was
all green and gold lying there dappled. The next
she was half-way up the lawn and in motion over the steps.
The door opened magically and she disappeared. She would
never wonder about anything, just say, 'That spoon needs cleaning.'
And yet I think it means she needs remembering.

Malcolm Working

Malcolm is working. That is, I suspect that Malcolm's working.
The light in his room is on. The little Greek vase
Where he keeps his stray thoughts looks, even from a distance,
Stuffed quite full.

The world of the Classics seems intact, neat and confined
To dark, humorous people, deftly shaking from
The little Greek vase ideas, images, values ...
Old languages pulsate in the room though; vibrations

Like electrical spiderwebs cross between the houses
And end up in the dishes and bubbles of my kitchen sink;
I hate to take out the stopper; what's running down the drain
now is Malcolm working while I'm working.

A Page of Rage

'I saw how to pow him out.'
Susan running at night comes in the door at high speed
and slam temper, flushed, with eyes unnaturally bright.
The object of her rage was some guy at the bus stop;
he said something objectionable, she doesn't quite remember what,
but it reminded her of incidents way back in childhood:
of being strangled in her scarf till her eyes popped,
of being tied round the telephone pole by her mitten strings,
of having her boots taken off and filled with snow,
of being whipped by a dead snake in the laneway.
It reminded her of entering rooms and being ignored,
of long vigils by the telephone.
                                  'I suddenly realized,' she says,
now having gotten her breath back and being matter-of-fact,
'When you get mad you get awfully strong.'

The Blue of the Swimming Pool

The blue of the Swimming Pool isn't a real blue
And there is no easy way to describe it as water;
It transforms an ordinary backyard and the ordinary people
Who roar up in trucks, sitting stunned for a moment
Now that there is no longer the moving belt bearing them on;
Getting unbelieving out of the trucks, setting up playpens,
Getting undressed and into bathing suits and finally entering
The Pool.
   The Cat sits (while no one is looking) on the portulaca
In the rock garden and looks at the people in the unbelievable
Not real blue of the Swimming Pool. There are the very young
Grandparents, their own married young and the spouses
And the assorted babies of the married young. Muscular,
Shining, joyous, the babies unafraid, they all accept the water
Moment: fountain of life or very womb.
         And the Cat looks on
In the sharp sunlight and drinks in at the eye the not real blue
Of the Swimming Pool and the swimmers transformed and moving
Freely, ordinary and beautiful.

Little Anne Running, Big Anne Shopping &
Another Anne's Mysterious Visiting Birds

Little Anne runs from flower to flower to flower
honey-haired happy every minute every hour.
Big Anne shops successfully and hardly stops.
Another Anne's house abounds with the evening sounds and even words
of mysterious visiting birds.

*

Little Anne tosses sticks into River Thames
this is one of her camping games.
Big Anne reads on the beach and lets the waves reach her.
Another Anne says, 'Well Polly how pretty you are.' and 'Just
listen to that canary up there.'

*

Little Anne running, Big Anne shopping and reading on the beach,
Another Anne tending her mysterious visiting birds;
These Annes appear in different strips, unknown each to each,
so make their first acquaintance here in a blur of words.

Lost Everything, Almost Everything

Poem (with Canadian Reference) from Anne Sexton's Letters

    Black Wed., Belgium, Sept. 4, '63

All belts lost for both of us which makes everything unwearable:
Gone the umbrellas
My blue & white stripe sleeveless dress that I wore in Canada so much
My navy heels, both sizes,
My navy clutch/two pair of stockings
Shorts, shoe polish, orange jersey blouse,
Lost everything, almost everything:
The navy low-cut, the aqua two-piece, the silk aqua print,
the white arnel print sleeveless,
the navy knit with white and kelly green top;
Slippers,
All underwear except for extra pants,
hankies,
two bathing suits, much less ten copies of my books;
                            almost everything:
(I didn't lose new poems in mss for they are in the briefcase.)

    Black & White Thurs.

Went to the Flea Market (like two rather old & wrinkled Perry Masons)
to spy out our lost clothes.
                      (Not good detectives we lost the scent,)
but, true women, we did find: something to wear:
laid out on old bedspreads on a pile of really dirty old clothes
a fine-looking houndstooth suit, very Peck & Peck, and fits Sandy.
For me, for the Poetry Festival Ball, blue sixty dollars,
but it can't be helped   lost everything

      Silver Sat. eve.

We are supposed to be at the Ball.
To hell with the Ball.
The dress I will wear on New Year's Eve.
                                  and you
Will fall in love with me. That's
What I want the dress for.
                    Almost everything lost.

About Noon

    About noon
when the whistles blew with a cockscrow I came
out of the grey granary of the employment building
      onto Spadina,
at that point wide as a barnyard.

Truckers were unloading chickens in crates,
        redeyed scrofular
chickens much as children there with their beaks agape
to know they would be sold with fishes out of
        clearwater tubs,
hard naked as stevedore loaves and warty old vegetables.

The february sun shone typically toronto
        in a trickily gutter,
made a ray in my eyes like murine, all straw
coloured was the widewayed city then and a barnyard.
Over the bakery leaned a woman with a broadshawled bosom
          letting her son's name fall
from the windowsill. He came then
          applecheeked, coalheaded,
rushing along with his shoulders bang and check
(see he'll grow up a character from Aucassin)
           a puddle jumper and his blue
            zipper jacket rushing too;
There was a downflash of a dime for bread.
I thought this was the real colour of the land—
and had a Golden Goose flown over Kensington Market
with an egg for every pousey pocket,
        they were that gay.
I saw the overall factory workers through their cellar window
          drink a bucket of coke
            heard a joke in a strange tongue;

This was the real Canadian farm atmosphere of the golden age
the bee, the threshing where no methodist had been ...

There was the engine roar of the team overhead on the barnfloor
                                                they were drawing in
while we sailed shingles on the cold green horsetrough
                                                        and were children then
and as innocent of the power of horses that's a city's harnessed power
as of that point where the quick quiet sight of sun on water
                                                      starts to make this poem.

The Tin Shop

The Tin Shop never sounded tin
it sounded canaries;
because of the Great Depression
no one wanted eaves
but everyone wanted canaries.

It became the place where
                     we changed skates
sharpened them
traced out our initials
on the floor,
sipped cocoa.

The Tinsmith bred canaries
that lived in tin apartments
elaborate as palaces
spacious and filling all
the upper air
with communal soprano.

The Tin Shop never sounded tin
it became a meeting place
for men
displaced workers
all their strength now
gone into those deep voices
vibrantly disaffected
politically haranguing
words/scored as deeply
in the wooden floors as
our skate blades.

The canaries sang and moulted
a world of yellow.
The men's words, strong,
bedevilled, are they in the
end gone like the
songs and the feathers?

A Tree for St. T.

o green
green St. Thomas!
with verdure so bosky, with
coppery beeches that sheltered
a Prince: with ginkgo, magnolia
and sycamore dusky, with
chestnuts for parklights in
michigan park: with pinetree
and fir tree, with strong
oak for doorslabs
for dark ancient
houses, secure
from the threat
of indian
hatchet &
socialist
pamphlet

*Inwhich I Realize I Meant To Clean Up My Brother's House
As A Nice Surprise For When He Came Back
From His Camp And That I Have Left It A Bit Late*

Ah Yes, my Brother's House / the Many Mansions of.
: Kitchen walled with two-month-open Clarks Beans Cans
: green moss Everglades Fridg Door
: rainbow Jungle Band there little Bathroom
        (tidepool Washcloths ebbing into Labour Day)
: stripped, blipped Bedclothes (mats
        bureau-drawers spilling their dry Niagaras)
: Blinds, frowsy-eyed Windows accusing: *You left before the Dawn!*
: foldback little Bedrooms, unwrap-you dust, down pouse
        and dust-mice down, summer-chasers!
: O Empty Aquarium   O discarded and chewed-at Dog Collar,
burnt-out *Wintarios,* (numbering beyond our ken
lost week-ends by the bushel), fish-hooks, guitar-picks,
the snapped string, the cracked lens
: Cellar, damp old Picasso dreamland-you of the sardine-can (shucked,
swept and hilled), Comic Book Valley and To-day Mag Alley,
dune centred Auction Sale desert sandings,
Varsol & stripper Hoardings in Crown Imperial quarts squandered,
scuttled wringer-washer parts shifting, vying
for Frogman's coming,
Lianas, vines of the lines of the leotards parted, struggling out
(jammed hinge on the Treasure Chest) /out/
            built black as earth's bottom,
            Incandescent garden full fall
            Dahlia, Ontario.

The Dieppe Gardens Poems

Eugene and Peter read their poems
about Dieppe Gardens, Windsor,
a September evening, once, here in London.

Dieppe Gardens, it's not a park where I've walked,
but I remember the news of it coming—Dieppe—it came over the fences,
(field by field, farm by farm): 'bad news from home.'

Someone called and we would leave off hoeing,
go to the fence, and there, crying or trying not to cry,
a Windsor girl asking us to pass bad news along

though all the lists not in ... We threw ourselves at the ground,
and that day passed, (half-hope half-fear) as if just striving
might somehow balance out the half-knowing.

A time of drought: the fine dust caked our hair; our cracked
hands, blunt fingers scrabbled to put right
a bent plant; all was more bitter-precious on that day.

Evening came; on the gravel we walked barefoot, asking,
(field by field, farm by farm), could we use the phone,
but nothing changed: only 'bad news from home'

day halved slowly into night.   Your words,
Peter and Eugene, go active into memories long stilled,
and I am filled with wonder for the walkers there
        in Dieppe Gardens now.

Sociable People Wondering What I Do

Sociable people wondering what I do
Sometimes ask me, 'Do you ride?'
'I used to ride,' I tell them.
At that point it is difficult to go on:
The cruel War was raging
Coventry Cathedral, Londoners
In the Underground, Dresden, the North Atlantic and Dieppe:
All that I rode through; some I realize
Wouldn't call it riding at all what we did,
Five years of thundering about on gravel roads,
The terrible energy biking out to the farm,
Dawn and evening, and obsession about the right horse:
The dust and fervour of our adolescence; madness and
Danger we must have ...

*

'We must have been crazy.'
(hospital held-down, she still laughs the same,
the vibrant ghost, pale, stroked,
the broken hip poorly-set, the ever-present
cigarette jerked toward her mouth, a pain jerk;
she who never jerked the reins.) 'Do you remember how
Crazy we were!' It is all coming back, the dusty roads;
Laughing, choking back laughter so the nurses won't come
(and teachers won't and parents won't). 'I got thrown so many times;
why did I break my hip going to work?' Unanswerable.
(the break is an old one
but how long has she been in that chair,
that brace, that walker ... how long has she been in that chair?
Suddenly I can't figure out my own set ways.)

'You were crazy. Do you remember the last time
you rode? We came to a jump and you couldn't
make your horse go over; you got so mad you

just got off and that was it; you never got on a horse again;
I remember because I had to lead them both back;
you wouldn't even touch the reins.'
After all these years she has the same explanation:
'You were crazy.'
     We are laughing again.
     We are bothering the patient
in the next bed. (She still laughs the same;
she sleeps little
she does puzzles in her head at night and has for years
she lives on 222s and *Craven A*s
and she is crazy about her youngest son especially
she is always eager to talk about the old days).

For nothing in that ordered hospital room
Has any meaning to explain it all:
       the years,
The dust and fervour of our adolescence,
The madness and the danger we must have.

      *

Sociable people wondering what I do
Sometimes ask me, 'Do you ride?'
'I used to ride,' I tell them …
At that point it is difficult to go on,
Not as it was before
   (different now);
Now I can hear her laughing, coughing, pale and stroked,
The vibrant ghost, jubilant:
'Do you remember how crazy we were!'

The Tomato Pickers Observed

Civic Holiday—1981—St. Thomas

The block between Ross and Moore is still torn up for the new drainage system so that the whole busload of us is disembarked in the wasteland at the rear of the Bus Depot. Charterways is not unkind—that's how it is:

The Queen Anne's Lace growing by the tracks droops a bit forlorn in the iron breeze. The gravel moves, shimmering illusion, just slightly in the humid air.

Despite the holiday, construction men are working, but slowly; moist and damp, the distinct smell of excavation and possible Legionnaire's Disease wafts over from Talbot St.

Naturally the Bus Depot is closed up—tight.
Tout fermé.
The Tomato Pickers have about an hour to wait for the Leamington Greyhound, but they don't know that, nor do they know where to wait.

Like a digger's load of fetid earth and gravel, the rattle of the Driver's parting instructions; the small stones of his staccato English, received full face, have now covered them.

They are still monuments sitting on their suitcases, smoking feverishly, red-sweatered the women. Man Statue leaps up, tries to get across the chasm of Talbot St. to the closed restaurant and the only visible comforts tombed away.

But even as I leave them, the Tomato Pickers have that slumbering energy of the temporarily entombed. They burn with avidity and fervour for the tomato, love apple, with a primitive instinct for dim-remembered fields.

As even after the holocaust, language unusable, stiff-boned, laughter and energies benumbed, the Tomato Pickers of the earth will rise, picking their way out of the rubble; small people, incomprehensible to most, battered suitcases clutched; enduring.

Beatie's Palaces

'Jeez, you got good leaves,' says Beatie.
Leaves are her luxury; no trees, no leaves on the cinderhill
where she lives by the dump.

> Mother Madam Witch
> wind lashes trees for her
> we all fall down

Without asking she grabs the rake; she eyes
our corner lot. Beatie is by far the best raker, maker;
her house begins to grow, a rich emerald carpets
every room. 'Thirteen rooms maybe,' she says tersely,
'anyways a room for each of you.' Palaces
are what Beatie makes, raking.
And I can still see, squinting through a chink of time,
Beatie's hands, short-fingered,
(chipped, the polish on her nails, but she's 'allowed'),
her short, strong hands lengthening fiercely into our rake,
small lady of the strangely long arm, she manoeuvers
right round the corner onto East.

'I sure like your leaves,' says Beatie.
Grade Seven will be her last year at school.
She flies around, adjusting the wind-bruised walls;
her red sweater is nubby and too small,
her skirt hitches up, her legs are chapped,
her pushes are energetic:
'In there. In. And don't come out till I say so.'
We fall separately onto our too-short leaf beds,
try not to annoy Beatie, amazed and proud
she likes our leaves.
What did we dream of there on Beatie's palace beds?
Infinite luxury, oriental harems,
we drifted, anticipating,
the leaves rustled innuendos about Beatie's mother,
infinite luxury, oriental harems ... Abruptly,
'All right, you can come out now.'

'What's for supper?' one of us asks audaciously.
'Macaroni with catsup,' says Beatie positively, 'and don't ask
for seconds, because you'll get none.'
We look with respect at Beatie, who hands out leafplates
in the big kitchen room. Even the kids taller than Beatie
look with respect and envy at the short, leaf-stained fingers
and the ruby glass ring—(she has privately 'promised'
it to each of us 'if we are good');
Beatie doesn't shift her ring around, finger to finger,
about thirteen, she is already married to life.

*

We got called in to supper
to do homework
to practice
to get our hair washed.
Beatie didn't go home till it got good and dark.
Beatie didn't have to.
She raked by streetlight with a harp sound attached to the long arm.
We missed it when it stopped,
for it had gotten into our blood, the idea of Beatie raking, making.
From the window (a last look before the wind scatters),
there is Beatie's palace glowing gold and green.

>Mother Madam Witch
>wind lashes trees for her
>we all fall down

St. Thomas: the Great Heat Wave of '36

anyfool wd know it wd have to be
a muchlessfargone Head
says my Mother, fanning, rocking, speaking
elliptically of a Lettuce

Anyfool (I) sat panting, flushing, sweating
getting geared up to go back to Loblaws

the Neighbour Boy, just happening
to hear (permanently Glued Ear,
Eyes rivetted on our Verandah)
twigs, speeds, delivers:

Word goes out, o the da dit of life,
all the wide world joins now gossip glee
And the Black Spark tells it
far and near, dooms it fast down
& into the Drowning Pool.

*

Commiserating strangers pause
coming from the market, one
foot on the bottom step, shift,
shuffle, old smalltown natural
piety Interest evident
(their identical faces meanwhile siesta,
in their shopping bags)

* *

& so my Mother, rocking, fanning
& so my Father scanning surreptitiously
Greenwood
& so my Brother teetering, toppling, waiting
Dick Tracy on
& so the Baby (benefitting by stepped-up fanning)
& so I, holding dejected, rejected Lettuce Head
(gaining breath for dipsy-doodle back to Corner)
So we all partook of the Great Sad News:
puffed, panted, sweated out
dropletted on our bottom step:
That the Heat Wave had finally got Old Ed
down at the Corner, won't be
the same—everyone knows—
just can't believe it—
saw him downtown only last Wed.

Inwhich I Become Confused, the End of the World Being Imminent

They say the world's near ending and this confuses me. I've a mad desire to try on everything in Eaton's. I rush there as fast as I can pick my way through the rubble; far away on another street the buses are still running. Eaton's has lost part of its roof, but the escalators still bear us upward. Passing me, going down, is the Wife of the President of the University. She nods encouragement to my smiling mouth (shaped into a 'hats?'), to my two big Ohs of eyes. The staff is putting all to rights though a stiff breeze from the roof area nullifies their efforts; blouses move on the racks like sailing ships eager to leave port; in the Shoe Dept., a Clog Dance;—they are thinking in Promotions, thinking, and soon there will be a Special: the Super End of the World Special. I hope it won't get going till I finish my shopping.

Was that what I came for? Shopping? The pink-orange neon of a truly beautiful sunset pervades the Lingerie Dept. I feel we are part of an ad lay-out; I dart among the shoppers; we seem happy to be there.

'There's no coffee. They have no water,' I hear a slightly familiar voice saying as I enter the cafeteria. 'They have Coke.' With coke and biscuits and cheese I too am quite contented. I puzzle about where the voice belongs in my past. Just trying to fit a face to the voice will keep me occupied for quite some time.

Parody 1: Margaret Atwood, 'Presolstice'

The cold wind rises around
our house, the wind
drives through the walls in
splinters; it is time to put away the garden tools.

The folding chairs
slip easily into one of those
large leaf bags. Two will slip
into the large bag. The ordinary bag
is too small for both of us,
my gentle husband and myself.

I dream of departures, meetings,
repeated weddings with a stranger, wounded
with knives and bandaged ...
I climb out having forgotten something:
to clean the garden tools etc.
and spray them well with Pam. They
will not rust over the winter.

Nor will my husband for I spray him well
and close the ties;
after all he has the company of my head
in the bag, eyes closed
and snoring refrigerator snores.

'You will find that the folding chairs will slip easily into one of those large leaf bags, often two chairs will go in the one bag. Clean your garden tools etc. and spray them well with Pam ...'   Reader Exchange, *Toronto Star*, Oct. 4, 1980

Parody 2: Raymond Souster, 'The Worm'

Don't ask me how baby managed
to corkscrew his way
through the King St. Pavement
(of his nightie)
I'll leave that to you.

All I know is
there he was
circling, uncoiling
shiny little bottom first
wiggling all ten toes
(and I had followed directives
for using three strips of masking tape
instead of those nasty pins)
yet there he was
as the warm rain fell
out on King Street
in early April.

'To keep baby's open-backed nighties together, try using three strips of masking tape. Baby does not feel the tape ...'   Reader Exchange, *Toronto Star,* Oct 4, 1980

Parody 3: W.W.E. Ross, 'There's a Fire in the Forest'

There's a fire in the freezer
The milk cartons are melting with
The flames close behind
With the ice-cubes driving onward.
From chicken casserole up to
The high crackling health foods
The fire's surging forward.
There's a fire in the freezer;
The whole fridg is burning!
The whole world is burning!

'To defrost a freezer, use a hand hair-dryer. It will defrost in 10-15 minutes....'   Reader Exchange, *Toronto Star*, Oct. 4, 1980

Parody 4: Al Purdy, 'The Rattlesnake'

An ominous length uncoiling and thin
A sliver of Satan annoyed by the din
Of my ten fingers with just one intent:
To get it remeshed, this damn zipper that's bent.
It should move without motion, it should hiss without noise—
Just rub with lead pencil, and O Joy of Joys ...
No, it eyes me unblinking from planets unknown
As alien as Saturn, immobile as stone.
No hint of expression, no trace of regret, no human emotion,
                                          recalcitrant, set,
Just rub with lead pencil before I forget.

'If you have a zipper which does not slide easily, run a lead pencil up and down over the teeth.'   Reader Exchange, *Toronto Star,* Oct. 4, 1980

Parody 5: Phyllis Gotlieb, 'Ordinary Moving'

Here we come on our plastic slipper feet
Maw she makes them and makes them neat

We sing from near, we sing from far
You brought us here, and here we are

You take the milk bags three to a pack
You slit them from the front to the back

We sing by night, we sing by day
Nobody told us what to say

You rinse them well and you let them dry
Your maw can make them if she'll try

We sing from far, we sing from near
Nobody told us why we're here

Just save those bags and you'll have a store
Of plastic slippers, that's what they're for.

Here we come on our plastic slipper feet
Maw she makes them and makes them neat.

'The plastic milk bags (3 to a pack) can be used to make slippers for those who like to go barefoot and still keep their feet clean. Slit tops of bags. Rinse well and dry. Cut down each side 4 inches or 10 centimetres and cut off upper flaps. By saving these bags you can always have a store of disposable slippers.'   Reader Exchange, *Toronto Star*, Oct 4, 1980

from the planned woodlot to the freedom of Mrs. Field

1. The Planned Woodlot

   The planned woodlot
   where we are the only things that move:
   ('and since that day no bird flies over Glendalough'
       —the Wicklow man telling it all in the bar
         this comes again where no bird flies)
   and we are trees, tourists,
                                an air of wonder prevails:
   the voice that stills the waters
   (that floats there Players and Sweet Afton soft)
   that is the bird
   the bird that never sings
   the song getting lost, you and I
   drifting through the planned woodlot.

II. Into the Trees

'dear woods I know them all ...
                         the day
when I have to leave them my heart
will be very heavy.' Ah yes, Claudine.
Above my head the porcupines steadily munching chips,
on the edge of Grogan's old clearing a deer
poised leaf and silent in the glades
as sound of paper (pencil on)
pages,   leaves falling,
through the grey-brown shapes of sound
& the imperceptible drawing back of the bow.

III. Going for Water

    Then the only sound in the August clear
    is Carmen Sim's pumphandle
           creaking thirst
    drawing it up, the Crystal Kingdom,
    and we are going for our share
    and we are crossing the back line, worsted,
    gravelly and lately corduroy,
    and we are feeling smoother now satiny
    slipping over the weathered log bridge
    tinpail aswing in our two hands,
    and our bare soles touch down to August
    and the big Grayling swish under the bridge.
    Smooth, clear, we laugh once over,
    twinned hands divining that instant caught
    when someone somewhere is Really Praying.

IV. The Freedom of Mrs. Field Out Divining

It sprouts in seasonal mist,
the feel of the gold drawing, burning.
Under the crunch of crackle snow
deep buried
but twitching the locket pendulum.
From reefs of packsnow
newfallen (feb. southwind)
   sinking her snowshoes
   settling;
   should she slacken
   go slow step
      to waterlogged settling
      and sleeping
      and reefed
      white in the whitebush
      slow sink of the deepdrifts
      newfallen southwind
          she drifts;
     does not slacken
        ongoing
          her pace never varied,
    never quite over the gold, but
    the freedom of Mrs. Field Out Divining.
And we divine her, plumpish
Ordinary Mrs. Tom Field of the patient eyes.
Instant pendulums of the heart
twitch, twig, tell us:
   Don't ever stop now, Mrs. Tom Field, but
   stop or not,
   all the gold under all the bush in the world
   it's only in that heart of yours, only
   in the freedom of Mrs. Field out divining.

The Martha Landscapes

1 *the alternatives*
   to stay
   to go, a straight path into the future
   the Beloved Face carved on the rock
   here and there couchant pines
   at an absurd angle
   how they would cling
   the Living Head

2 the Bears backed us into the Cave:
   I thought fast in my dream, tried to push the children out
   (my children, Martha, Martha's children)
   through, saying: Dive or climb down.
   We heard our children falling.
   Disciplined, Martha obeyed—a straight path into the future.
   My brother didn't budge, sharpened a stick,
   we burned what was at hand, a 1936 newspaper,
   then rammed the short blaze at the snout
   and the axe to the skull
   the bear only staggered.
   Meanwhile I searched out water falling
   held up my hand, pressed my cheek different directions,
   felt the slight suck of air from the dark corner.
   She backed off and we heard
   the cubs scrambling, falling
   as the rockslide now choked up the entrance.
   'You scared her off too quickly.'
                                    The alternative ways out:
   water sound, chinks in the roof,
   down in the harbour they would see our fine smoke filtering,
   Martha swimming, swimming bonechill
   now just seal or gold-eye
   having her own dream in the blue waters.
   Twilight now and the fishermen turning back.
   Fog would steal over and mask the headland
   she would swim on and on and reach the lighthouse,
   remembering other islands she kept on swimming

perhaps she missed the pier and slid up the coast
came to where the Stewarts fished their breakfast,
perhaps kept going through Georgian Bay
ghost paddlers, speleologists,
under water she would rest in those caves rarely visited
maybe she portaged
overland to the Red River
maybe a friendly icefloe landed her on Baffin.

'I hope Martha makes it,' says my brother.
Instant acting, he has grown up in his mind.
In the future he searches out his Air Force Manual,
sat studying it watching the dying fire;
I checked out two tunnels
reported back nothing,
my sweater was almost unwound;
'That was not so smart,' says my brother. 'You'll
need it later if we get separated.'
'We won't get separated.'
Just then the bear worked free,
backed out whimpering
great shoulders pulling free
entrance crumbled;
first we rushed forward
then back into tunnels
fire out
a roar of small gravel danced the fire out.
He kept the flints
I remember they cut my hand.
More air, then rubble—no air.
There we sat—
he was five years old, I remember,
and our blood rushed all over rose quartz
my yarn threads wound round us, binding us together.
'We'll have to move this mountain,' I remember him saying.

* * *

Martha went on; she climbed shale sidings leaving
half her palms behind till she was striped
all over like bacon, barefoot and light she went.
Her palms sprouted in time stigmata,
great trees cranberry-coloured bore arterial fruits,
sent out space-signals so that strange saucers landed near her,
she saw Excalibur flashing on their instrument panels;
                    They picked her up, took her away,
China, anywhere;
                    She worked her way back as a nursemaid
for some people going home—they went aboard at Capetown—
she was capable and the children charming,
they called in where outriggers came out with fruit
brown river water joined them,
The Empress of Australia, 1900, finally docked at Southampton;
all the while Martha was troubled trying to remember something
all the years in the big country houses, on the staircase descending,
the children dressed to put in an appearance for a few minutes,
punting, teaching them to swim ...
The river was clogged with reeds
there were no visitors
it was hard to meet anyone
they were all at War;
The game-keeper getting caught in the poacher's snare
she freed him
she tore off the hem of her petticoat
and they bathed his ankle in the river,
went back to the punt,
she carried him into the kitchens and they sent for the doctor,
old, he came in a trap—he had served, my God he had served,
a naval surgeon, rum on the wounds—
all those legs, English, French, German into the boiling sea.

                              *

Martha lived quietly in the 'cottage for life'
helped the family then worked on the land.
Eventually in her old age she decided to emigrate
she came in at Halifax and crossed the prairies with the war-brides
—she had a very strange feeling she was going home.

* * *

Down there all one
we heard the train passing far away
stopping
'It's spring now,' I would say. It's later
warm water crusades onto our yarn-wrapped bones.
We don't care.
We play at being born.
Groundhog scuttles near our air holes
crimson the sumach and later skies all Canada blue.
Now spring
small hepaticas where the cave roof fell in
where the Indians still come, place their fetishes.
We hear foghorns autumn evenings.
Walkers on the trail pick blackberries
lean over and start landslides.

I am comfortable
moreso in the springtime than just previous.
We hear far down the splash of oars
the small clip of oarlocks
hear mother's voice counselling patience
hope of fresh fish for breakfast.
We let the fog lick us all over
now that we are born.

The Artemesia Book

Name Dropping As Skipping Stones

On the edge of the Huron water a father is teaching his son to
skip stones. He bends, crooks, casts. It is an ageless teaching.
If I were close enough, would I hear him naming them all, wishing
them a long life of dancing, in the way my father taught us to
name the stones? (By the feel in your hand you divined the various
uncles, the various neighbours. Of course our acquaintanceship
was small, but as well-known as if they were part of our own bodies.)

*

Thus, with a lobbely stone it was Great Uncle Mark making it to
first base on his wooden leg and one of the little ones on his
shoulders. 'Bert's my navigator,' he always said.

A truly flat, light shard was Tillie Weaver, operator at the
telephone exchange. She was rumored to have skipped fourteen times!

*

Now I'm turning these memories into skipping stones, thinking
I can feel them in my hand this moment of naming them, letting
them dance again into the waves:

Dear Frank Scott, appraising Susan, and saying, 'What a neat little
Guide.'

Margaret Laurence, shining up Adele's bathroom very early in the morning
(without making one sound of taps), and later explaining, 'I think
it must be the Puritan in me.'

Marian Engel, eyes glowing, saying, 'This looks like a perfect
snowdrift to make an angel,' as she was finding her ride.

And Milton Acorn, maybe thinking of himself as a lighthouse,
fog-horning 'Colleen, you must stop living in Queen Alexandra's time.'

Listening in Together

It's a very thick atmosphere this night.
It's a dark chocolate cake of a night.
It's so dark out there you couldn't find a lost friend
If you had lost one.

     I have run out
The kitchen radio on a tenuous black thread of extensions,
Now it's playing Beethoven, something I don't know:
I am preoccupied finding my book, switching on the porch light,
Getting the couch cushions arranged just right.
Once lying down, my eyes are on the silver body
Fat, determined Music Treader of a most ordinary moth;
Level with my face he starts his climb, slow keeping time,
And a far more dedicated listener than I, his thin legs
Delicately cling to the screening, perfectly listening,
Perfectly moving upward.   Entranced together
Up we move with the music, moth and I,
Concentrating as if we were present
At the original composition, determined
To see it through.

     And he does reach the screen top,
Balances, stays, as the radio plays on. Listening in
Together, the back porch light the one star,
In the very thick atmosphere this night.
It's a dark chocolate cake of a night.
It's so dark out there you couldn't find a lost friend
If you had lost one.

     Before I fall asleep I think
My Music Treader sends me a message about a lost friend:
I see again the beautiful Luna sipping
At the sugarwater we left set out summer nights
On the bedroom window ledge.

Childlight Town

My eye goes out clear as a peery
Clickets a little getting started
—Like Stepping over a star—
And then falls down to Childlight Town.

I get back beside the bleeding heart bush
By the whiteporched house where it all started:

My Grandma laid her square Scotch frame
Resolutely down among the tall-cut dandelions.
The half-hour we watched the Owen Sound road
No one saw us that went by.

We looked up at those fat green stars that
Are maple leaves and make a Princess
Out of just a plain tree. The air
Was as blue as a blue glass cup and as clear.

One day, she said, I will not make a hot dinner;
We'll have bread with brown sugar on
Out under the Duchess trees ...
I wonder what they would say to that?

If you are a good girl, I will give you
That little brass donkey bank,
But if you carry on the way you have been lately
When I ask you to pump a little water why ...

She would give it to one of the boys.
She would also give a piece of her mind
To Mr. Cherry one of these days who let
His heifer stomp on her geraniums.

I reflected how my cousins
Were all common as English daisies
And that I should look down on them one day,
Safe in the arms of Timothy Eaton.

They had no friend as I had Constance,
Pale as her own canary bird
Because she was dying of consumption
And was twenty-seven years old.

Nor had they ever been born out of the empty air
As I had onto my own arm,
One of those celluloid windmills held out of a
Car window and all whirled up.

On hearing the first car turn in my Grandma,
Smiling like a Lady Sun,
Got up and ran to put the potatoes on.
I streaked for the barn to get to the playhouse first.

They were all piling out, the daisies,
Yelling that I would not go to heaven,
And that they were coming to bust my dishes up
Though my aunts said to stop that sort of thing.

And really I wanted them to come that day in their stupidity and beauty
And break all of my dishes into pretty little-sized pieces of glass I could live by.

Inwhich I Put On My Mother's Old Thé Dansant Dress

'Yes,' said Janos, 'you can put on a costume!'
So I go for a favourite, my mother's old thé dansant dress,
(black georgette and hand-made lace). When I was a child
I looked through snowy windows, seeing her leave
for 'Tea For Two'. Leaves whirled, the hem dragged
in the mud when granddaughters sortied out for Hallowe'en;
and then I rescued, laundered, aired and pressed
(black georgette and hand-made lace). Now it's a humid Sunday
in the scorching summer of '88. Jamie retreats to the doorway.
Janos, taking the photos, says, 'Nearly done now.'
I think, my whole life-span is in this dress.
And, as I strew these words,
rose petals are falling from the matching hat she made.

Lines Not For Mona

Reluctant weeding out
as if the years were protesting such dispersal
and memories saying, we're still petalsoft:

I've saved the last crispy carnation
from your Mother's Day flowers, son.
And I twirl it between palms
divining how our lives have spun since
day of miraculous-emerging
of your small red head,

and I think I am looking now
into the whirling heart of the flower
with the intent bright eyes of your own small daughter.

Photo

Amy, Benjy, Marian are on the beach.
Behind them the blue and silver boat
Lulled on white sand waves
… ripples of joy … they are floating.

Up there in the sheerest blue
the camera is just another gull
swooping in, fixing their fluidity,
calling: 'little cousins on a summer beach,
let me keep you here together;
let me brush your smiles forever
with my soft feather of joy.'

Amy, Benjy, Marian are on the beach.

Watermelon Summer

'Going to be one hot summer for sure,' said Uncle Willie
who had set his heart on growing watermelons
in a cindery patch at the very end of his Garden.

'No one is going to look there for them.' He told no one
but us, planted them at night. Joyce and I
biked sweatily out to our first job, tenderly

moved translucent baby cabbages, made little hats
for them, carried water endlessly and longed
for the promised crisp bite, the pink juices

reviving, 'turning us into real people', he said.
We were just at that turning point, thirteen years old;
we dreamed of the watermelon promise.

He said they were 'coming along nicely', green
taut, bulging over the hillside, as yet
undiscovered by the boys.   September came.

The boys came. One Saturday morning we saw
yellowing leaves only and every watermelon gone.
Yet the anticipation of the melon miracle

seemed to have turned us, Joyce and I, into 'real people'.
And we pondered this, purposely noisy with our milkshakes,
solacing ourselves with second best.

Miniatures

I I look through a circular window:
   I make a frame of small twigs with budding leaves;
   Inside this the first spring skippers are jumping:
   Yellow and pink, yellow and pink.
   The soundless rhythm of their feet jumping
   Becomes visible as bubbles on this cup of tea.

II The grass-seed sower casts, casts,
    And behind her the birds come
    Greedy for her hopes. They are eating up
    This poem almost as quickly as I can make it.

III The long-legged man is again whistling
     As he goes early to work.   Seen
     Through a basement bedroom window,
     he will always be recalled by boots and jeans,
     and the whistling that encircles him completely
     in his day's dancing.

IV Anne Brontë's grave is planted completely
    and mysteriously: 'No one knows who tends it.'
    This time it is lined by yellow pansies,
    and fixes (for a short spell),
    our hammered-by-the-sea-winds straying thoughts.

V 'The little island of the year,' my mother says
   and so from desert island it grows;
   populated by family: Family Reunion. Disquiet
   about estrangement motivates roots-out-of tumbleweed:
   annual habitation (strangely)
   magnets from a tiny stamp or the kiss
   that fixes it on the 'just-a-reminder' postcard.

VI Kathleen Raine's red leather writing-case
isn't a notebook; perfect copies only:
'The function of it is to invoke the Divine Presence.'
The word torrents flow at last into a calm pool,
(the British Museum Reading Room) and my desk
floods red as Canadian sunsets, as that cover of leather.

VII The Birch-Bark-Biting-Artist-Woman
(called less wonderfully Angelique Merasty,
and it's called Wigwas, what she does),
takes a day and holds it up to the sky:
checks, folds, bites ... and suddenly
there is a pattern of butterflies and flowers
(or of birds and star shapes)
on the monotone, anyold, birchbark day of the week.

VIII Ian writes: 'hills rise suddenly and individually
out of the plain; the landscape that looks
so unreal in Chinese paintings is
actually that of the countryside.'

                              I reply: 'I feel
I want to wave back at you from this shore.'
My hand grows into an enormous
golden chrysanthemum.

IX Last night I dreamed again about being a bread pudding
lost in the forest.
In my bones I feel every jounce that my Raisins take,
(rolling to a safe spot); every Pinecone becomes the Enemy;
every clump of Ferns rattles my Eggs and Milk;
every Stone I come up against fractures my Bread bits.
I wake up, much depleted, fetched up in sunshine and hornets
against a friendly stump.

x Again in the British Museum Reading Room:
   (though I have gone down with the Camden Town mystery pip),
   hoping for my return they put out the Elizabeth Jennings Box:
   (lampdustmotes aren't the incendiaries of her schooldays); her works,
   in air/motion from other tables, (liberated-
   out of the vault), vibrate, stir: I am here!

Inwhich I Meet The Strawberry Shaman
And The Japonica Bushelful Bountiful Lady

The Strawberry Shaman wears a strawberry-coloured caftan
and the hem gleans dried grasses and clover as she walks;
her conjurer's toes in the Cloudwalker sandals
should be sending out runners into the fertile ground,
but into the near-desert chants of Odemin, Odemin, Odemin
are cast like spent seed.   Strawberry Shaman doesn't believe
any more. 'You see,' she carefully explains: 'When Star Radiance
is the name for an eye make-up ...
                                        When Rainbow is the code name
for a secret police operation ...
                                        When Sun on the Snow
means a nuclear disaster somewhere, then
it is time to stop believing.'

Meanwhile down the street the Japonica Beautiful Bountiful Lady
has been too busy to keep up with the latest news;
it has taken her two days to fill her house with japonica.
Every available container has been pressed into service:
thirty milk cartons march up the stairs;
the bath and the sinks are full of red and falling splendour.
From her window at night, she sees the world
framed in japonica, and she caresses her palms
with satisfaction mindless of the countless tiny stigmata
set up by japonica thorns.

Inwhich Tim, Bill and I Discuss The Governor's Road

Hi, Tim and Bill, this is not turning out exactly as I meant it;
but, like Jeanette and Inja, it is well off (or on from)
what *that* book is recalling about the Governor's Road, O.K.?

I thought about its building, but all I could hear
was the train churning and Geza saying: 'Textures,
textures; we're into the textures now.'   He was

keeping himself awake drinking Via coffee from
a plastic triangle, (bruising to the lip), courtesy
Amenities Canada for the coach class.

His eyes got shinier, blacker ... his words sledged
out like rolled-over stone ... but he never slept
from Montreal to Union, where out he jumps

helps me with the baggage, and I help him out
at the Canada Trust./Forsythia he breaks off
ruthlessly, whistling, rushes away up University

Avenue./The next time I hear the textures
song: 'Textures, we're into the textures now.'
is in a Grade III in an about-to-be-closed school

in North York, where they have pushed away the desks
and made a circle and are stamping out:
'you are the Top Banana' with a good mix of faces/voices.

('O, that's nothing, Colleen,' says my mother, (who
had gone down to help out Sheila with her Grade III's
the Easter before); 'Why, they told me *I* was the

Top Banana *three* times. Of course, I could really be of help;'
(referring to her elevation to pupil-teacher
in the Model School in Belfast, circa 1910.)

'I taught them the *roots of words* and to chant
the Alphabet. They won't ever forget that I
was there. Sheila said that I was the best.'

So much for an M.A. with McLuhan, crosses
my mind, ... lucky thing I took along my old
Roller Disco hat and could play marbles ...

'Yes, mom,' I yell into the phone when she
takes a breath, 'that's what I want
to tell you! They asked about you ... the girls

wrote you a group letter. I'll bring it over ...'
slightly mollified, (the brogue softens), Bell clicks along,—
I listen and roll the sole of my tongue, scuff

it back and forth, listen to the rustle of dry poplars
torrent of maples and birches, thrashing down;
Chop, swing, chop;/malaria and corduroy:

the branches of my thoughts turning to ash;
the fine houses following us along with instant
English gardens; cruel schoolmaster following

with his cane. (The soldiers chop ... the squatters
all are chopping, burning up the slash). A young
Lieutenant leaves his heart in a pannikin

of spring water ... Sunbonnets and birch switches
and 'Texture, texture, texture, texture'
of the brown eyes watching them.

from Throgmoggle & Engestchin: A relationship

Inwhich you meet Throgmoggle & Engestchin and you may feel that the latter is not a fully developed character and you are probably right.

Throgmoggle Fordful
manty overgoo
bog manty gong goppling
rill cum nack throggins.

Choomin:
Chillchinchar Engestchin
chanty chopcharchill
chorey chopcharchill chooley
chingle choon chingley
choodle.

Throgmoggle Fordful?
Chillchinchar Engestchin?

Fulford mog-gle throg
Throggins
Besaboom
Besaboom
Throggins
Manty choon Manty
chorey manky
manky minsteven
Besaboom chorey
Choodle chin chin char
Gundalling tandy
Upert bee neery
Upert a choodle,
Laddledy leery
Upert a choodle
Nin Nin Nin

Besaboom chorey.
Powdler
Blanko
Upert a choodle
Nin Nin Nin
Manky Minsteven
        loppleton leery
        laveling,
        limpeling,
        leddledy lumpoling ...

Fordful moggle
chorey chumbles
dipdum danker.
Engestchin chuh
chuh
ch
h

    *

Para pom
tandle:
Chillchinchar Engestchin
chanty chop charchill
chorey chop charchill
chingle chun chingley
choodle
        ooldum.
Throgmoggle Fordful
manty overgoo
rhinger minsteven
bog manty gong goppling
rill cum nack throggins.

Para pom tandle.

Throgmoggle & Engestchin & the Bird People

Inwhich Throgmoggle and Engestchin spend an Evening with the Bird People and hear of varieties they never knew existed.

Throgmoggle.

Engestchin.

        Bally Buddness.
Bom Bom Bink
Rot Tellinga
Bildy Engel
        zing zong ziller
        jim jim jillny
        lirr lirr lirr
        lufson lilter
        lodlaw blanco

Throgmoggle choodle
          upert a choodle
Engestchin zingly guppins
        zoopins
        zally
        zloor
        chyty chawl

        O
        lir lir lir
        lotsun
            oolah zimble.

Throgmoggle & Engestchin, Having Read the Reviews

In which Throgmoggle and Engestchin are Expecting a Light, Refreshing Comedy.

—Alla zing zimble?

—Calla oolaa??

  Para chuff chuffins;
  Zimble chuff chuffins.

Poola cartin …

galla cum paddla!

        Manty obah glumm
        oordy!   oordy!
        Besaboom obah glumm
        zattir chuff chuffins
        zattir zing zimble
        oordy! oordy!

        Mordy manty
        maldy mordins
        inkle pardy
        inkle luff.

Pally Pally.

Throgmoggle & Engestchin Experience An Upsetting Border Crossing

—Engestchin, wullum rallda?

—Bop, Throgmoggle,
bin bop alta.

Paddin ockle?

bin Paddin ockle.

Punda.

Tam unden wacky

olin *besaboom*

linty linty.

Punda.

Tam unden wacky

olin besaboom

linty linty.

Paddin ockle?

bin Paddin ockle.

Mardy pad mardy

rel pan an pan rel.

Nin Nin Nin

                Engestchin

Besaboom.

        Para pom

    tandle.

Wild Turkeys

Fall season, the russet trees blending
into a Tony Urquhart bird.   A pheasant
big as a house prises off the storm windows.

Groggily I struggle up from the couch, blinded
by the shattering colour (I have been slipping
alternately into Morley Callaghan, 'sweating it out', and hacking

up great litres of souwesto phlegm), go
to the window, stamp and clap and 'shoo' (shout)
as to a wild turkey, trying to remember

what it was my Great Grandfather, Sandy Stewart, told people:
'It's easy. Birds talk the opposite of Fish.'
Or is it the other way round?

Fanning Mill Into Shredder

Ascending, I meet Nida on the stairs (she's coming *down* from the Chambers)
and, between coughs, try to tell her, ask her,
pointing down at the Old Farm Machinery Exhibit,

about does she know anyone who knows *how*
(and to tell me about it) *how* to turn an old Fanning Mill
into a Shredder?? 'I can't figure out how to do

the teeth,' I gasp. Scythed off, my lungs rattle and laugh
and I am torn between me lying in the ditch/toppled
November scarecrow and me winnowed/winnowing

out the chaff beard awn. Meanwhile,
quite a bunch of Sunday people want *down.* Down
from Jack they float, beatified. *Descending.*

Race Track Kids

They are c.b.'d in the trailer, the day I visit
(those 'measle-pink specks' in reality, but it is chicken
pox), the kids. 'Not good here, but better than Florida,'

says my cousin Pete's wife. The trailer is spotless;
they are lying in their bunks, keeping out of mischief.
'So long. Get better soon, eh.' We stand outside in the mud.

I hop from one foot to the other trying to keep warm.
Amber rain falls with a cold sound (the reverse
of fire snap) of persistent rusty-nail colour ...

twisting nails, it is hard to get the words out,
(what I have to tell my cousin Pete) ... finally, 'My boots are leaking.'
'Come into the stalls,' he says; 'it's warm by the horses.'

The Cooper

Brian puts out the barrel for the Fall Clean-Up
and I rush over to it twice. I feel over practically
every inch of it, weathered as the space round

the knot-hole (stretchable) where we teetered over the not-enough hay,
surveyed the world. I though covetous
cannot roll it home, as Jamie would object.

And Brian says: 'Well, it's no good, is it? The bottom's
sprung and the wood's thin.' In the night (waiting
to hear it roll away), I dream of my great-great grandfather

(apprenticed to a Cooper), after fourteen years finally getting his scrip
and walking north to look at the land, and meeting the two Americans
who said: 'It's no good. It's under water.' And walking south
      and apprenticing himself for another fourteen years.

The Belfast Policeman

Salmon, 'monster salmon' swish through my memories
of the Ulster grandfather's story; a policeman from Leitrim, he fished
'monster salmon', thereby eking out his pay. And all grew brainy

on his catch. A few soft childhood words for ease of netting, harsher,
of course, for those who drunkenly swam up the Belfast gutters,
sobered the night away in the quick-vacated

beds of his sons, my uncles. Through the years we fed
on the Ireland of his fishy tales—never saw *him*, banged my spoon
in Chesley till Granny thought of another. My brother

stirred at the breast, sucking in milky salmon stories. One
evening my grandfather, the policeman, feeling 'a bit wearied'
lay down before teatime 'without taking his boots off' and died sudden
    and quiet in Welsh.

One-eyed Pierre

My sister gives Susan a cryptic message (late picked her up
at York Mills and parachuted her out here at the 401 in the rain;
coughing she walks a mile to the nearest bus-stop) ... teeth-chattering it out:

'Tomorrow. One o'clock. Behind the Bull Dog Steel.'
She is talking about the rendez-vous for the 'Re-enactment'
at Thamesville, what our family calls Moraviantown.

—That's where One-eyed Pierre met the Middaughs, at the Battle.
—He had fought in Seven Wars. —He could shave in the dark.
The sort of story, once heard, gave me the ancestral migraine

and a lack of trust in this left eye of my own; it keeps
wanting to scout out invisible territories, knowing everything
about surprise attacks and the cold, cold rain.

This Dragon Year Will Eat You Up For Sure

This Dragon Year will eat you up for sure!
I unscroll it from the Fortune Cookie while the waiter watches.
Once on D'arcy Street, sitting on James' steps, strumming away,

a little illegal runs over giggling: 'My grandmother
says, tell you, you have Chinese mouth, always talking or eating.'
Much pleased, I chord: 'Thank your grandmother very much from me.

Tell her, she is a good house-watcher too!' Sun and dust
choke me but I keep smiling.   In another city Liang Jun
comes like a humming-bird on her bike. 'I am coming

to help you, Mrs. Reaney!'   She has left *her* grandmother
'in the mountains', always carries her photo, smiles,
says: 'This Dragon Year will eat you up for sure!'

What Happened to the N.Y. Sunday Times?

A hot Sunday in August. Jamie has a virus, and I wonder what
would *I* like to lie and flop with, and I think: It's the N.Y. Sunday Times!
It's heavy and my soles burn, but I make it home from Shaw's

(along with milk and red-pail-full of Camay bargains
from the Big V), braving hornets, Sunday joggers ...
waving to Charles and Father O'Keefe.　　　Jamie seizes

the Book Review Section all about big '89 Rimbaud
Year coming up, and I am left with Carl Lewis
being 'the one' and that maybe (just maybe) Business

Ethics might come back. In the night, fuzzy-headed, I roll
off the back-porch couch and sleepily find myself peeing
into an 'After The Fall' bottle. And in the morning,

fogged out by another night of unbearable heat and noise,
I wonder: 'Hey, what happened to this New York Sunday Times?'
　　　　　　　　　　　　I have gone a little over.

Running Down To Barachois

Summer, and my sister has this idea of going to the East Coast
or, as she says, of running down to Barachois.
Her old neighbours, the Cormiers, leaving Toronto,
have said: 'for sure, come anytime. You step
out the back door into the sea.' Tempting, this magnet
destination, but we don't get our compasses boxed
till Quebec City, running down to Barachois.

So far we are mainly running down to discos
and visiting with the street artists but—the telephone
number is found. Jubilation! It is answered
by a Cormier daughter (the one who is married
to the man with the English name, something
like Penny) and we do get the Box Site number, essential
for running down to Barachois.

The daughter (married to the man with the English name
something like Penny) has said that her parents were out, but
'for sure come anytime', and my sister divulges
that Mr. Cormier drives a Humpty Dumpty Potato Chip truck.
This makes our shopping more confident, this thought,
and extra boxes are with us, waiting for the after-midnight train
at Lévis, for running down to Barachois.

Extra boxes, angular paintings, these didn't make us the strangest travellers:
The James Bay strikers were there, hefting their foot-lockers,
muted by their Union men, and all of us deferential
to the draped coffin of a famous river pilot,
Captain X, and his cortege—all these bound
for Gaspésien villages, while we run down to Barachois.

Sitting up all night in the coach, our heads packed square
by our many boxes … 'It is their virility,' says my sister
as the James Bay strikers board like maddened bison, then
crouch along the aisles … 'It is their freedom.' Freely, their tears
are fresh as morning dew when they see the old cars waiting
at the stations. They step out into the sea.
While we run down to Barachois.

We miss their virility and their freedom, the James Bay strikers,
when on the Moncton platform at last we wait the Humpty Dumpty truck.
'Rusty from Juniper Junction', balancing seven 'on sale' lawn chairs,
tells us Trudeau will be passing through, scoffs
(she says) a leather ring from my sister in the confusion
of Trudeau actually taking a very vigorous platform turn.
While we run down to Barachois.

There is no answer from the house where you 'step
out the back door and into the sea' (even from the daughter
with the name like Penny). 'Rusty from Juniper Junction'
gathers in his seven 'on sale' lawn chairs, that had waited
like a delegation for Trudeau … There is no Mr. Cormier
in his Humpty Dumpty Potato Chip Truck.
As we run down to Barachois.

But the hotel is lovely, super. We sleep deeply after the night coach.
So far my sister is mainly running down to discos.
I try out the vernacular with the women who run
the chewing-gum and newspaper cash-register.
'Yes,' they come from Barachois, '$20 a run.' I mention
'La Sagouine'. 'La Sagouine est morte,' they insist darkly,
(meaning the real one), as we run down to Barachois.

'$20 taxi each way! No way!' says my sister, who has met
a Cement Plant Inspector at the hotel disco. He
has to turn in a car at the airport, but will take us
bright and early to the Box Site. Better, we find
a small Post Office in the General Store. 'O, yes!'
they know our Cormiers; he drives the Humpty Dumpty truck
and they have gone off to Toronto ... as we run down to Barachois.

'Why did they go to Toronto?' asks my sister. 'They
couldn't wait to leave there.' 'To see old neighbours.'
I visualize the Humpty Dumpty Potato Chip truck wending westward ...
And the daughter married to the man with the English name? (It *is* Penny.)
Once a week she comes for the plants ... She lives?
'O far away.' We leave a note for the Box Site, climb into the green car
of the Cement Plant Inspector. As we run down to Barachois.

The Cement Plant Inspector leaves us at the airport.
Our Taxi Driver (with plastic flowers framing his licence)
is, of course, a Cormier, and tells us: 'Come back. Come anytime.'
Next time, for sure, it's the Humpty Dumpty Potato Chip Truck
that will be waiting to take us to the house where
you open the back-door and step into the sea
when we run down to Barachois.

Looking At The Artemesia Book

Sometimes I wonder whether I am the last person left alive
Who started school with a slate and slate pencil.
First thing we had to break the pencil in two
And give half to our neighbour
In the double seat.

Our teacher assured us there would be paper
And pencils before the snow flew.
We clinked open our empty inkwells
And looked enviously toward the big kids,
Watched them dip.

The rows between did have pencils, did have paper;
(The School Board was proud if poor.) And the clear fresh air
Of Artemesia 'sharpened our wits', free to all
Though especially to us beginners whose seats
Were by the open windows.

Out there moved the tallest treetops in the bush
Down in the valley. Out there were birds and fish
In the creek. Fallen from innocence and freedom,
We gave it all up for the shriek of slate pencils
And the dizzying waves

Of an ocean called The Written Alphabet that endlessly beat
High round two green walls, carrying on where blackboards
Stopped. (Being the shortest, beginners printed THE LITTLE RED HEN,
Standing under the small chalk showers of the taller ones, reaching
Their ornate Spelling Lists.)

From the first day accidents punctuated the even drone
Of the sounding out and the counting on fingers. Our slate-water
Bottles rolled and shattered; hornets got in, but we bravely
Kept on singing O CANADA; 'Lift up your feet!' for nearly
Every day ...

'Someone is peeing,' loudly whispered my seat-mate
And sure enough we watched the amber stream approaching,
Quite approving that boys from the outlying farms
Would never trust those toilets in the basement,
Sinister and ugly white.

Soon the shut windows were painted with a silver forest.
Soon just coming to school, walking behind the plough and keeping
Our schoolbags out of the drifts, became more important
Than school itself. We were so matted with pounds of packing snow
That we rolled back down

The hill (all the beginners), missing the bell, supreme
In a resurgence of innocence and freedom (that one day),
And only struggled up to meet recess coming out
And the bob-sleigh being manned, and were kept in
And thawed out, and so missed

Seeing the bob-sleigh smash into the doctor's car
And the Entrance Class killed.   Blood on the snow (I saw it)
When we were carefully dismissed and thought, it's like
The abattoir. When we came back after two days
With no school,

It was as if we were not the beginners anymore.
We looked up thoughtfully to make sure it was still there:
Yes!   The endless dizzying ocean called the Written Alphabet
Was beating high round two green walls, and it became our solace
For a little while.

Notes

Sea Gone Girl: Except for 'Amethysts,' 'Butterfly Window' and "'It is a rainy day in March,'" which were published in *Air* 14.15.16, the poems in this section appear for the first time in volume form.

My Granddaughters Are Combing Our Their Long Hair: Poems in this section are drawn from the volume of the same title published by Coach House Press in 1977.

Ten Letters: First published by Nairn in 1975, this was the concluding section of *My Granddaughters Are Combing Out Their Long Hair.*

The Martha Landscapes: Published by Brick Books in 1984. 'About Noon' is chronologically out of phase with the poems in this section, having been first published in 1949.

The Artemesia Book: New poems. 'from Throgmoggle & Engestchin: A Relationship' originally appeared in *The Martha Landscapes,* but here joins its near relations. 'Photo' was set for two voices, and 'Watermelon Summer' for clarinet accompaniment, by Jack Behrens. They were performed in London, Ontario at Trillium Plus, '89. 'Childlight Town' was first published in *The Canadian Forum in 1949.*

Colleen Thibaudeau was born in Toronto and has lived in Grey County, St. Thomas, Winnipeg and now London, Ontario. Her books include *My Granddaughters Are Combing Out Their Long Hair* and *The Martha Landscapes*. Her poems appear in many anthologies.